# JIGSAW

## Putting The Pieces Together After Divorce

By
Mindy L. Hitchcock

*with*
*Joel S. Gehrke*

# JIGSAW: Putting The Pieces Together After Divorce

This book is intended to help people going through, or recovering from, divorce.

Published by:
Mindy L. Hitchcock
20700 Civic Center Drive, Suite 170
Southfield, MI 48076

ISBN:       1-4196-6352-6
EAN13:      978-1-4196-6352-9
Published:  January 7, 2008

Published in the United States of America

10  9  8  7  6  5  4  3  2  1

Trademark Acknowledgements

LADY4JUSTICE®is a trademark of LADY4JUSTICE PLLC and/or its affiliates. Outlook and Outlook Express are registered trademarks of Microsoft Corporation. All other brands, products and company names mentioned herein may be trademarks or registered trademarks of their respective holders.

**Contact Us**
Contact the authors at  info@lady4justice.com
For Free Email Tips, and the Electronic Version ("Ebook") in full color Adobe PDF format, please visit www.lady4justice.com

## Acknowledgements

This is to acknowledge the people whose contributions took this book from vision to hard copy:

Joel S. Gehrke worked enthusiastically to make textual corrections and stylistic contributions to this book.

Martin Trautschold (www.blackberrymadesimple.com): I gave you a simple Word® document. You skillfully added beautiful pictures, and affirmation boxes with aplomb, thereby turning my 1's and 0's into a book.

Vaughan Davidson (www.killercovers.com) My killer cover guy. The day I looked at your cover, I realized "I have a book!" It was like welcoming a new baby.

Barbara R. Peter's skilled and diligent editing efforts brought **JIGSAW** into its final civilized state.

Tara Katchaturoff made valuable stylistic contributions to the final version.

## Dedication

With all my love, I dedicate this book to my twins, Alex and Alexis Johnson. There is no one on earth as precious to me as either of you are on your worst day. Since the day you were born, my desire to make you proud has inspired me to accomplish most of whatever I have done. I hope I have succeeded.

Love, Your Mom

# Table of Contents

# About The Author

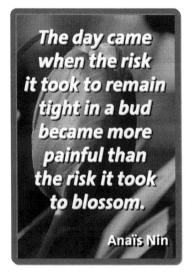

*The day came when the risk it took to remain tight in a bud became more painful than the risk it took to blossom.*

**Anaïs Nin**

Mindy L. Hitchcock is a lawyer, speaker, and author whose passion is to be a beacon of healing through love.

As a divorce lawyer, Mindy works within a social context that almost always involves pain and loss, and is supposed to involve bitterness as well. In these situations, Mindy has developed a holistic approach which transforms relationship breakups into life breakthroughs.

After living through her parents' breakup, and then her own divorce, Mindy suffered financial challenges and the loss of self-confidence which often attends life wrenching experiences. Refusing to be defined by her circumstances, Mindy pursued an intensive course of personal development and gave herself to study of spiritual teachings. Along the way, Mindy derived valuable life lessons that brought her to a new level of personal fulfillment. In finding her own comfort in this "dark night of the soul", Mindy also discovered a passion to give healing and empowerment to those going through divorce.

For Mindy, it all comes down to the acceptance of a few simple truths:

We are 100% responsible for everything that happens in our lives.

What we send out comes back.
What we believe about ourselves becomes true for us.

The fruit of this inward revolution is a no-nonsense, proven methodology that has helped many clients discover the unique contribution they came to this world to make. For Mindy, that meant the founding of a holistic law firm, Lady4Justice PLLC, and later, the presidency of the International Alliance of Holistic Lawyers (IAHL). Looking back from a standpoint of several years, Mindy now knows that struggle is the opportunity nature gives us to find our greatness.

Today, Mindy helps people who are struggling with negative self-image and a lack of motivation, achievement, and dream fulfillment. She writes a monthly column for a national newspaper, *PhenomeNEWS*, and her self-help website, www.mindyhitchcock.com serves a worldwide audience. Says Mindy, "I believe we teach what we need to learn, and by helping others, we ultimately help ourselves."

Moving through fear and self-doubt to success and joy, this book reveals Mindy's insights, derived from her challenging journey through divorce to her own, now extraordinary, life.

# Introduction

"The world's a stage," mused Macbeth, "and every man a player in it." When Shakespeare's play begins, Macbeth is a decent, dutiful, military officer; but he allows himself to be convinced that he has no responsibility for his own choices. As the story unfolds, this single false belief transforms a noble soldier into one of the saddest characters in the canon of western literature.

It's reasonable that a great playwright should see life through an actor's eyes. For a student, a novelist, or an artiste on the banks of the Seine, fatalism presents an all too convenient escape; besides, it sounds so worldly and *savoir-faire*. But as a single mother, a lawyer, and an employer in the workaday world, I don't believe that my life is someone else's script. I create my life, every day, and I am personally responsible for everything that happens in it.

As I have found it, life may be better compared to a courtroom. Every day we plead the case for our own happiness to a Universe that is infinitely fair. Unlike a mortal judge, the Universe has no bad days. It consistently and impartially reflects back to us the fruits of our own beliefs.

Every day of our lives, a conversation takes place within us. From this place inside, we are constantly sending out thoughts which create our lives. So it is that our thoughts blossom into words and deeds with creative or destructive force. Just as the farmer can only harvest the crops he has planted, the only fruits we will see in our garden of Life come from the seeds we have sown. What we send out comes back to us. What we believe about ourselves becomes true. By whatever measure we give, by that measure we receive back again. There are no exceptions.

This is universal law, and knowing it is the path to power. It is good news, because acceptance of this reality gives us infinite power to create the lives we want. It is also bad news because, unless we take steps to actively change our thoughts and thus our world, we will just keep getting the same old thing. Garbage out, garbage in.

In my journey, I have found that insights do not necessarily follow a logical sequence. Wisdom arrives in fragments and flashes over time. After my own divorce, the pieces fit together (as one might expect) piecemeal. Over time, it was those little flashes of insight that lit my way to a new life.

In this book, I share what I learned about body image management, finances, dealing with the calendar (aging, that is), relations with my children and my relationship with myself. It was by making small changes in my beliefs in these areas that I ushered joy back into my life after my divorce. These chapters, and the affirmations and sidebars included with them, are a guide to help you forge your own path. I condensed the learning that occurred for me over years to enable you to benefit from it *now*.

Michelangelo, the Renaissance master, was once asked how he was able to bring such beauty to a plain marble slab. He responded, "I do not create the statue. I merely see the statue that already exists within the stone, and remove the excess."

From the method of Michelangelo we learn a simple, yet profound, truth: Within each of us, there is a masterpiece; unique, extraordinary, and beautiful. The way to discover it is not by adding to it, but by letting go of the things that hide who we truly are.

This is the magnificent, first, true thing about you and everyone around you. You are that block of stone; that, and much more: You are your own Michelangelo!

It is not daily increase, but daily decrease, that matters. As you release more and more of the old beliefs that do not work, you will get in touch with your own inner power, and the masterpiece will begin to peek out. In time you will see your own true Self, and then you will find that there are no limits.

It is my intention that this book help you on that journey. Your passion is waiting for your courage to catch up.

In love,
Mindy L. Hitchcock

# 1: Speak With Your Own True Voice

In my vocation as a lawyer, it is my job to speak for others. It's a job I enjoy. Outside of court, though, I speak up for myself. This not just a privilege, it's a basic human right. When I exercise this right, I feel good. When I fail myself in this respect, I end up failing others too. I cannot love my neighbor unless I first love myself.

You care about people, and that's a wonderful thing. But as you plead their case, remember: You're a "people", too.

"Be courageous, it's one of the only places left uncrowded."
Anita Roddick

## Speak Up for Yourself!

I used to get up at 5 A. M. every day; exercise, review a case, and rush to the courthouse by 9. Returning to the office, I would meet with clients until 5 P.M.; then help my children with homework in the evening.   In between, I might console a friend undergoing divorce, or email a note of support to another friend applying for a job.

Often, in the middle of the day, I would long to get alone and read a book; but the responsibilities I had accepted into my life left little time for such a luxury. I accepted this responsibility because I was doing what I thought I was required to do to be a good person. Then one day I went to a retreat, and heard a speaker whose words jolted me to attention.  She said that if we were compromising our own long term welfare because we couldn't say "no" to our family, our boss, or our friends, we had become a help-a-holic. We needed to stop, breathe, and honor ourselves. Whenever we smother our inner voice, we suffer. When we speak our truth, we win.

Have you ever attended a funeral for someone who died of breast cancer? Did you not find it crowded with people who spoke of the dead as if she were a saint?   It has been observed that women who contract this terrible disease are often the kind souls who nourish everyone but themselves; the kind who says "Yes"...to everyone but herself.  And so she passes into the mist, a martyr to the family and the obligations left behind.

Dr. Christiane Northrup, a physician and author of several books about women and health, describes the need to be a relentless nurturer as the "Burnt Toast Syndrome."  If a family come to the table for breakfast, and a slice of toast is burnt, who ends up with the burnt piece? Mom!

11

Take an example from the ordinary affairs of life. Before an airplane takes off, the flight attendant will say, "In the event of cabin decompression, put your own mask on first before trying to help others." Why? Because you can't help someone else if you are suffocating. You must love your neighbor *as* yourself, the Bible says. Most of us read that as "Love your neighbor." But what is implied is "Love *yourself*."

In a 1998 movie titled *Living Out Loud*, Holly Hunter plays a character named Judith Nelson, who gives up her dream of medical school to marry a cardiologist. In doing so, she loses all her friendships and everything she has known to become the supportive "doctor's wife." Fifteen years later, when her husband leaves her for a younger woman, a pediatrician, Judith is left to confront some unpleasant truths about herself and the compromises she has made.

At one dramatic moment when the couple face each other in an elevator at the lawyer's office, Judith tells her husband: "I don't hate you for leaving me. I left myself long before you did." Taking personal responsibility for her life choices, Judith opens her heart, and rediscovers the feasibility of her own dreams. Ultimately, she goes back to medical school and achieves her own triumph as a doctor.

When I was in my twenties, I attended law school at my husband's direction, because he wanted me to become a criminal defense attorney. I didn't even want to become a lawyer. So, I entered the legal profession, but I was not successful because I was doing it for him, and resented the fact. When our marriage ended, I was left to support our children alone. Despite my terror at being the sole support for my children and myself, it gave me a chance to re-examine my values and my purpose in life.

Having been dependent on my husband for so long in so many ways, it was pretty scary to go it alone. I craved security because I doubted myself and no longer recognized the sound of my own voice. It took time to rediscover my own gifts. I began to see that I had traded my Self for what I thought was the safety of our marriage. This is something many women do.

There is an old saying: "There are two doors in life, one marked 'Security', and the other marked 'Freedom'. If you choose the first, you lose both."

As I sat among the crumbled ruins of my old life, I began to rediscover myself. Guided by the wisdom of such authors as Louise Hay, I started building a life that worked for me. As I did, I moved beyond legal texts and began to align my law practice with principles I believed in. The scales fell from my eyes.

When I was a child, going through my parents' divorce, I used to wonder "Why do I have such a screwed up life?" Now, as I began to create a successful life and practice, I realized the reason that my life had been so profoundly affected by divorce: It was my chance to rise to the challenges so that I could help others going through the same ordeal!

Once I aligned my career with my true values, my practice began to flourish. In a few short years my revenues increased, seven-fold. Expenses that used to fill me with dread were now paid, without a second thought. I put myself to the test, and learned I could trust myself. Best of all, I found the satisfaction that only comes when you are truly able to help others, something I'd never experienced in criminal law. I had found my dharma; my purpose in life.

Like me, your dream of new freedom through divorce will not occur overnight. Instead, you may feel helplessness and pain, and even succumb to a sense of victimhood. The trouble with being a victim is that there is no power in it. You are always at the mercy of someone else, whom you can't control.

Freedom begins with accepting total responsibility for everything that happens in your life. Once you do, you will begin to see things clearly. It is change within, not without, that makes the difference. By taking personal responsibility, you gain control over the one thing you *can* change in any situation: Yourself.

Divorce can be an awakening where family members pitch in to meet the budget and handle chores. It can be a time when ex-partners work to support each other's new dreams-- just because happiness is the goal. It all depends on how you choose to view the situation.

Through the pain and upheaval of change, remember to be kind to yourself. Take time for long baths. Play soothing music by candlelight. Cultivate a new exercise routine that brings vigor and creates feelings of physical joy. If you can't bear to take that much time alone, take the children with you for family swim night at the pool. Go ahead. The world will keep turning. Take time for *you*.

How do you start on a path of balance and fulfillment when the world knows you as someone who will drop everything for other people? It is simple, though not always easy. Begin by affirming, "It is easy for me to stand up for myself." Say it to yourself 300 times every day. Sing it in the shower, or use it as a mantra when you exercise. Change is as easy or as hard as you choose to make it.

## Self

### How Do You Pamper Yourself?

- Treat yourself to a massage.
- Buy a CD of angel music - like Angel Love by Aeoliah. Feel the angels hovering over you.
- Take a bubble bath, light candles, and turn out the lights. Play soft music in the background.
- Give out a great big belly laugh, for no reason at all. Continue for 30 seconds for optimum results.

Each of us has an inner voice that speaks softly in our ears – "Go for it – you know you can." We can speak on our own behalf with strength and clarity – not anger and bitterness.

The first time I ever said "No" to a family member's request for help, I broke out in a cold sweat. I was afraid that she would hate me.

But instead of giving in to the fear, I took my daughter Alexis with me to have our nails done. We laughed together for two hours. When it was all over, I acknowledged myself with pride: I had taken my first baby step towards recovering my own voice.

*Affirmation:*

**It is easy for me to stand up for myself. I can say "yes" or "no," to any request, knowing that honoring my dreams and myself brings more joy to the world.**

The decision to help another can be an exercise of personal power, not a constraint of obligation based in fear of loss. As you learn to love, honor and cherish your true Self, you find that you are even more of a benefit to the important people in your life than when you put yourself last. Be sure to acknowledge yourself at each step along the way. It makes the next step even easier.

# 2: A Time for Planting

*"To everything there is a season, and a time for every purpose under heaven,"* the *Book of Ecclesiastes* tells us. Seasons change as they do each year: Buds form, flowers bloom, leaves on the trees turn green; then yellow, red and gold; then falling, only to begin anew.

People go through seasons too.

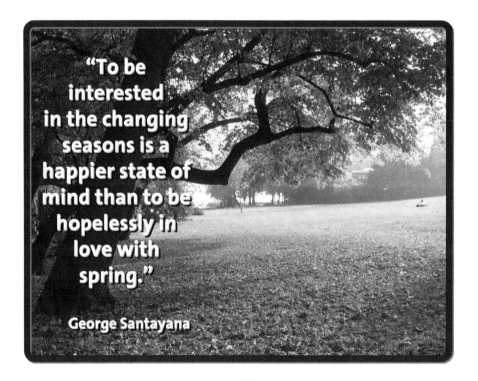

"To be interested in the changing seasons is a happier state of mind than to be hopelessly in love with spring."

George Santayana

## Seasons of Life

Often we expect ourselves to be the same every day, regardless of what is going on in our life. That is why we need to learn respect for our own personal seasons. Zen master Taisen Deshimaru says: "Some people treat their bodies like machines and try to keep them running indefinitely; then they wear out and cannot find their balance, and then come sickness and death."

Dr. Christianne Northrup, author of *Women's Bodies, Women's Wisdom*, compares a woman's menstrual cycle to the natural seasons. There is a "season" in a month when the woman's orientation extends outward to those around her. She expresses herself and gives. Then there is the time when she turns inward, and does her inner work and self cleansing. She may not feel like being social, or constantly on the go. Pushing herself to do so does not promote good health.

Seasons and cycles are how Nature progresses and we can see how well it works. We see it in the trees and flowers. Flowers start as buds, then burst into bloom and show their glory. In time, they begin to wilt, and then to die.

It is necessary for the plant to remove the old, dead flowers to allow the plant to put her energy into new blooms, which replace the old. Given the right conditions of temperature, light, and care, this cycle continues without end.

Cleary we, as part of Nature, go through the same process. Have you ever noticed that some times in your life are crowded with people and activities? Maybe you have children that keep you on the run. Maybe your work pace is frenetic. Then at some point you begin to notice that things slow down. Kids grow up, relationships end, jobs change, projects get completed.

Do you then feel that something is wrong because your life has slowed down? It isn't. It simply means you have completed one phase of your life, and that part has come to fruition and has been harvested. The next, seemingly dormant phase, is equally important. It is the time for planting new seeds.

This is the time for you to release old relationships that have become toxic. To let go of activities that are no longer fulfilling. It is not a time to rush into busy-ness; it is a time for stillness and nurturing. Use it to digest what has happened; what has served you, and what has not.

I remember times when I felt like I was in a cocoon, but I couldn't seem to snap out of it. I spent a lot of time in solitude, reading, meditating on what I had read, caring for my plants and animals. At that time, it was the only place I wanted to be. And despite criticism from others, I gave myself permission to be there.

When the time came to be active, I was able to step into the activities, composed, and fortified with the wisdom I had gained from my quiet times. Had I not taken that time for my Self, I could not have found the creativity I needed for the challenge that was to come.

Consider the Chinese bamboo. Its seed lies dormant for five years. During that time it must be watered and fed, or it dies in the ground. If properly tended, however, the shoot fairly launches out of the ground like a missile. There is no need for

---

**Taking Stock**

### Where Are You Now?

Take stock of where you are right now. If you are busy with a million things, enjoy the energy of this moment. If you are in a quiet time, take the opportunity to write a list of ten wonderful goals you want to achieve in the future.

Then, think of one thing you can do now to make them a reality. Start with baby steps and goals that can be easily achieved.

Once you take that step, plan another.

Remember that the journey of a 1,000 miles begins with the first step.

tending then; it will grow 90 feet in sixty days! The question is, "Does the Chinese Bamboo grow 90 feet tall in sixty days, or does it take five years?"

The answer, of course, is obvious. It took five years of tending to bring the seed to the point of sudden, explosive growth. The growth is impressive; yet the invisible, dormant period beforehand was absolutely vital. And do you not think that you are capable of even more than a simple plant?

In my law practice, there are times when there is so much to do there are just not enough hours in a day to get it all done. I may work late into the night, making sure everything is taken care of. And then the cases are completed, or something else shifts, and there is quiet time.

Having learned from my past experience, I now savor and utilize these times to their fullest, instead of obsessing about not being constantly busy. Can you imagine what it would be like if the phone NEVER stopped ringing? Of course we all love to welcome new business, but it is just as important to welcome the spaces in   between.

Slower times are a time for planting. In order to plant, you must first prepare the soil, remove the old debris, and make room for new growth. Whether you are considering a new direction in your existing career, new relationships, or a new direction altogether, it is the same. Slow times are the perfect time to explore your creativity. I spend my slow times writing or updating my web sites, something I love to do and rarely have time for anymore. I use them to explore new ideas I have wanted to try, or new places I've wanted to go.

> **_Affirmation:_**
>
> _I relax into the flow of Life, and see the good in each and every stage. I am at the perfect place and time for me._

There is an ebb and flow to life, and I am a part of it.  So are you. We cannot expect the waves to constantly crest; they must first subside and return to the sea.  Marianne Williamson says that we are like waves on the ocean, each of us thinking that we are different from other waves and not realizing we are all part of the same ocean.

Once we realize this truth, we need to accept and allow the natural rhythm of waves. We do not all "crest" at the same time.  We need to honor our seasons and get in touch with the power of stillness in motion.  This is when the Universal rhythm manifests itself; this is when we discover who we are. You can no more force yourself to grow than you can force a flower to bloom.  So don't try. Realize that you are in the right place at the right time, doing the right thing.  And so it is.

# 3: Give Peace a Chance

*Sometimes emotions like anger and bitterness cause people to take drastic action. But, the consequences of seeking revenge often reveal a price too high to pay.*

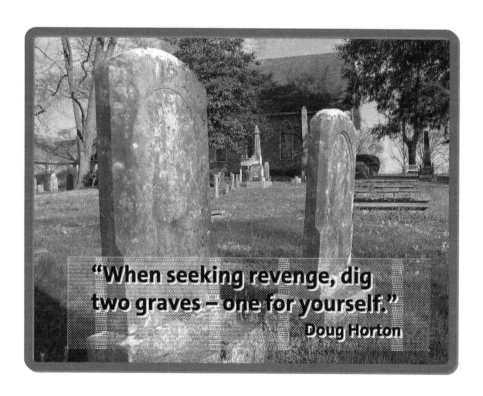

"When seeking revenge, dig two graves – one for yourself."
Doug Horton

## Reality Check

Divorce is official recognition that one of the most important relationships of our life has failed. That is why, no matter how much we decide to focus on the positive, it's hard to end a marriage without bitterness and grief. Recognizing that divorce is a failure, however, is itself the doorway to hope.

Helen Keller said, "When one door of happiness closes, another opens. But often we look so long at the closed door that we do not see the one which has been opened for us." My own mother never got over the pain of her divorce, and she spent the next 40 years in bitterness. In divorce, there is a compelling incentive to look backwards with animosity, rather than forwards, with hope. When bitter roots take hold, the ability to look forward is lost, and the healthy consequences of life changes are blocked. So the question becomes, "How do I deal proactively with the pain?"

In any marriage, there are wrongs on both sides. The problem is, when a marriage ends, people tend to minimize their own faults, and magnify their partner's failings. Nobody wants to be the cause of the breakup. Thus the tendency is to come away from a failed marriage with a sense of injustice. That is why it's so common for people to hire a contentious lawyer to punish their spouse, and heal their wounded pride. Sadly, a lawyer who chews up billable hours like a schnauzer on an old shoe almost never brings these goals about. Divorce can be a catalyst for an extraordinary life; but before anything new is created there is destruction. Reduction comes before increase of wealth, happiness, and joy. Divorce court is not a place to turn your sorrows into money.

Recently, a couple came to me to explore the prospect of a collaborative divorce. The man offered to support his wife and their child in accordance with standard guidelines tied to their incomes and future prospects. He offered to pay the house note until the child was grown. He offered to take all the parties' debts. The woman had an advanced degree (acquired during the marriage), a tenured position within a public school system, dependable transportation, and a beautiful house. But it wasn't enough.

For years, the marriage had been plagued by financial stress which had dashed their dreams and destroyed any hope of intimacy. At the end, the husband betrayed his marriage vows. The wife experienced a loss of self worth, and any suggestion of a collaborative divorce went straight out the window. She did not want to divorce her husband; she wanted to destroy him.

She hired a "pit bull" lawyer, who poured salt into her wounds and encouraged her to take a punitive stance. She was unwilling to share her pension, but she wanted half her husband's retirement account. She made an alimony demand that was ten times the amount recommended under the standard guidelines, and would have enslaved him for the rest of his life. Although she was dependent on her husband to pay the house note and her living expenses, she made it her mission to disparage him to his business contacts and to everyone they ever knew. Her own salary was used to pay her lawyer to run up legal fees. All the while, she was grieving because she was losing her husband.

When people use the courtroom to deflect the moral responsibility for their own heartaches onto their departing spouse, they don't really shield themselves from pain. They only postpone it. When divorce is viewed as a villain vs. victim exercise, there is no healing. Instead, the atmosphere of retribution destroys the foundation for effective co-parenting after the divorce. In one county where I work, 97% of the juvenile delinquency cases involve teenaged boys whose fathers were cut out of their lives in a bitter divorce.

In this recent example, the parties spent an amount equal to the wife's annual salary in attorney fees, appraisals, court costs, and extra living expenses over the course of the next year. One year after our first appointment, all the facts came out at trial. It was obvious that the husband's behavior had been wrong; but the court saw the wife as the "taker" in the marriage. The judge told her that she had gotten all the mileage she was going to get from her "victim" status, and had to enter an order to prevent her from further trashing her husband. She received no alimony at all, and she had to share in the repayment of the parties' debts. The husband ended up paying over $200,000 less than he had initially offered to pay when he and his wife first came to my office.

A battle between aggressive lawyers takes more than money. The highest toll is the emotional drain that the animosity brings. You and your spouse will stay angry with each other about the nasty conduct that occurs in a lawsuit, and it can take years to let go of the rage. Some people never recover. Sometimes there are scars visible in children and grandchildren fifty years later. And it doesn't HAVE to be that way.

Like alcohol or a narcotic drug, rage is both intoxicating and addictive. Feed it, and it brings destruction. Then there are the inevitable consequences to physical health. You can't work or exercise when so many endorphins are wasted, charging around like a bull in the ring.

I used to be one of those "pit bull" lawyers. I filed grudge lawsuits for my clients to vindicate the smallest slight. I sent out hundreds of pages of legal pleadings, to antagonize my opponents. Clients congratulated my tenacity, but inside I felt like raw meat pounded thin. I began to develop stomach problems. My family began to dislike me.

Looking at my peers, I saw that they didn't look altogether healthy either.

It's a telling statistic that lawyers as a group die twenty years earlier than their counterparts in the general population. How do I know all this? I was headed there myself.

When people use the legal process to give rein to their greed, or to exact revenge, they suffer the very injuries they want to inflict.

A friend of mine injured her knee in a car accident. Her husband advised her to go to an aggressive personal injury lawyer. "Great idea!" she thought, "That will pay for my master's degree!" And she was right. She made money in the lawsuit, but at what price?

That same lawyer recommended countless visits to the doctor, to bolster her claim for damages. She went, and she proved her claim. The result was a near addiction to pain pills and an overall feeling of sickness and depression. Because she couldn't be seen having fun in public my friend lost a year of cycling, bowling, and dancing. It would have detracted from her injury claim. Because she could not exercise, she experienced feelings of loss. For several years, she favored her other knee. When she gained 20 lbs., joy left her. But she sure paid for that master's degree. Yippee!?

For me, the awakening came in 1997, when I discovered a book by Louise L. Hay, *Love Yourself, Heal Your Life*. Then I went to one of her workshops. There I learned the law of Karma (and the Golden Rule) that what you send out, comes back. These are not just words. They are principles to live by.

I knew that I was not furthering the cause of love and compassion by hurling recriminations in court. In fact, that was why I hated the law, and my place in it. So, right there in that workshop, I decided to get out of law. At first, I tried teaching workshops based on Louise Hay's teachings. I did well, but quickly discovered that I could not support my twins with love offerings; so I looked to my inner wisdom for guidance.

Having learned that saying "I hate my job," only leads to another equally distasteful job, I realized that this was true of my attitude towards the law. I chose not to run away from the lesson I faced. I knew I had to start where I stood, and learn how to practice law with love. If I did not, how could I ever have anything to say to anyone about how to employ these principles in their life? Thus began my journey of bringing my law practice into alignment with my own principles and beliefs.

Holistic law is based on the fact that the best settlement is one in which everyone wins. This is not only possible; it is the only way to come out of a divorce with anything like a "win." Initially, colleagues laughed at the idea, but I knew that the Universal Law took precedence. It wasn't that the ends justified the means – rather, the means and ends were each points on a journey to enlightenment.

*Affirmation:*
**There is no revenge so complete as** *forgiveness.* **I** *forgive,* **and I set myself free.**

My intuition told me that there were many couples who come to the end of their road together and realize they need to move forward in different directions without acrimony. My heart told me that my client list would grow. To my delight, the quarrelsome, disagreeable clients left, and I began attracting clients who wanted to end their marriage as it had begun...with love. I began to love the practice of law. My life came into alignment with my beliefs, opportunities to talk about universal truth expanded, and I started writing a column for the phenomeNEWS, a local New Age newspaper.

In holistic marriage dissolutions, the goal is to look for a way that works for all concerned. This doesn't mean taking all or giving away the store. It involves integrity and cooperation to assure the finances have equity. More and more clients are seeking out this kind of service, because it is an honest way to end a longstanding relationship that started with love and high hopes. It's a way of respecting and honoring each other for the life you created together, and then releasing the past with love to open to wonderful new experiences.

A spirit of cooperation also makes it easier for children in divorce. It enables clients to co-parent successfully, learn their lessons, and move on instead of staying stuck in their resentments.

## Take Control Of Your Life

Take control of your life. If you find yourself obsessing with anger about what someone did to you, write an angry letter telling them exactly how you feel. Hold nothing back! Then fold the letter up, and write on it, "What I really want from you is your love and respect." Burn the letter, releasing the negative emotions. Don't send it!

You can also try punching a pillow or vigorous exercise to release your negative feelings. Emotions are natural and need to be released, not stuffed. Observe them, like the shadow of a bird flying overhead, not sticky but freely flowing. Remember, your emotions are not YOU, they are just a part of the human adventure. There is no one to blame, not even yourself.

We cannot hurt someone else without hurting ourselves. We cannot love someone else without first loving ourselves. Soon the entire planet will wake up, and all of us will rejoice. It is possible for everyone to win, but it takes courage to stay on the path, even when negative energy is hurled at us. And what should we do about the pit-bull lawyer? Send him some love...he needs it!

# 4: Clearing Your Space

*Your physical space is a reflection of your mental state. Create orderly surroundings by eliminating needless things, and you will reap the benefits of an ordered mind.*

"We need to find the courage to say NO to the things and people that are not serving us if we want to rediscover ourselves and live our lives with authenticity."
Barbara De Angelis

Do you want to know the state of your mind? You don't have to go to a psychologist for expensive testing. Take a look at your surroundings. What is the state of your home; your bedroom; your office? Look closely. You are seeing the state of your mind, projected before you.

Some people have to clear a path from the front door to the kitchen because their interior space is so congested. Do you see stacks of paper, books, objects that need to be filed, read or organized? This is the physical manifestation of the clutter in your mind. Do you see a comfortable space with plenty of room to walk, sit down, and enjoy your favorite possessions? External order is both the fruit and the root of inward serenity.

If you own up to clutter, now is the time to let it go. Just an hour or two a week spent de-cluttering will increase your sense of serenity. Start in one room and throw away twenty-five items you no longer need.

Whenever I faced a problem in my life in my journey after divorce, I found that de-cluttering often helped me find the solution. Once, I chose to start by clearing my home office. I threw away papers, files, and cases that had closed years ago. As I worked, I listened to Louise Hay's *Receiving Prosperity* audiotape and affirmed to myself, "I am cleaning out the legal files of my mind." In the process, I found a current file that I had been looking for everywhere, and another file that applied to a pending case. When the project was done, I had transformed my office from a foreign, chaotic place to be avoided into an orderly domain. The immediate reward was a feeling of serenity. I resolved to go forward, and as I de-cluttered my other rooms, I found lost addresses of dear friends, priceless pictures of my two children, even checks I'd never cashed. These items were dividends, but the biggest payoff was that by removing all the weight of useless material I de-cluttered my mind of useless thoughts about stuff that no longer mattered. I felt clear and open. I felt lighter! And I was.

In a Zen Buddhist story, a student comes to a master seeking wisdom. The seeker spoke endlessly about what he already knew. The master said nothing. Finally, he took the student's cup and began pouring tea into it until it overflowed all over the table. Still, the teacher kept pouring. "Stop!" the student cried. "Can't you see the tea is overflowing?" The Zen master replied, "Exactly. I cannot fill a cup that is already full." If we hold onto old experiences, bad memories, and the flotsam and jetsam of our waking lives, we leave no room for the new. Wisdom enters a clear space.

For years, I kept in my closet a horde of expensive high-heeled shoes. Some were brand new. I no longer wore the pointy, uncomfortable shoes, but I could not bear to part with something that cost so much money. I realized that the reason I hung on to them was fear that I would be unable to afford new ones to replace them.

> # *Affirmation:*
>
> **I greet the new with open arms. It is easy for me to clear out the cluttered spaces of my mind and open myself to the wonderful new experiences that await me, now.**

I took the shoes to a resale shop. The next day a woman stopped in who desperately needed shoes for her new job. She loved high heels. And so, I created joy for someone else. Soon my own closet was full of beautiful, new, comfortable shoes I loved.

As de-cluttering became an important ritual of my life, I found myself discarding videotapes I never watched, blankets not used, clothes not worn for years. My gently worn items offered new promise to the Salvation Army. Now, every six months I gather up at least twentyfive unwanted items. I repeat the declaration to the Universe: "I am cleaning out the closets of my mind." By passing it on to others, I keep the abundance flowing.

One person's junk is another's treasure. The *Dress for Success* program collects gently used work clothes from professional women and gives them to former welfare mothers who are re-entering the job market. The Salvation Army uses the proceeds from merchandise donated to its drop boxes and retail stores to help recovering alcoholics, victims of tornadoes and homeless people. When I help out, I have a feeling of boundless wealth.

It would be easy to hold a garage sale to get rid of all the excess stuff but I don't recommend it. If the focus is on clarity, prosperity and abundance, then giving stuff to those in need, has an expansive feeling. Selling good merchandise at a pittance creates a feeling of poverty and unworthiness. Cleaning out a closet and opening your heart brings an authentic sense of exuberance.

**Self**

# The State of Your Home is the State of Your Mind

For serenity and prosperity, gather up at least 25 unwanted items from your home and take them to the Salvation Army or another charity. You will free your house from unwanted items and help prosper the universe. Make a point of de-cluttering every three months, or whenever you want something new to occur in your life.

Light incense, play spiritually uplifting music, and ring bells (like Tibetan sound bowls) if you have them. Say "I am cleaning out the (closets, desks, refrigerators, etc.) of my mind." Bless the clutter with love and release it.

# 5: Take It Off!

*When I first began the practice of law, one criminal defense lawyer always stood out. While the rest came to court dressed in "uniform" shirts and ties, he would appear for jury trials in blue jeans! And because he was clearly being himself, people trusted him. Because he was following his own lights, he won the juries over. The lesson for me was simple: Other people know when you're being true to yourself, and they respect it. When you try to be something you're not, it's just as obvious.*

"Always be a first-rate version of yourself, instead of a second-rate version of somebody else."

Judy Garland

## Who's That Wearing the Emperor's Clothes?

When my twins were small, I used to spend money I didn't have to load them up with Christmas presents. I did this because I wanted to prove I loved them. Where did I get the idea that buying things was proof of love? From retailers and advertisers who bombard us with guilt every holiday season. What good mother wouldn't stand in line for six hours to buy a Sony PlayStation or this season's must have doll?

The belief that gifts made me a good mother is not all that different from the Hans Christian Andersen fairy tale, *The Emperor's New Clothes.* There, a gullible ruler really thought that some magical threads would help him gain respect from the people in his kingdom. And so he was deceived.

Two swindlers pretended to be weavers and told the emperor that they made the finest cloth imaginable. Not only were the colors and patterns beautiful, but also the garment, upon completion, was enchanted. Anyone who couldn't see its splendor was unpardonably stupid and unfit for office.

The emperor, being a little low on self-esteem, thought a new outfit would improve his stature and help him weed out unfit subordinates; so he paid the tailors a handsome sum to start stitching. The con men set up two looms and pretended to work vigorously. Meanwhile, the emperor was anxious to assess progress, but nervous he might be judged stupid if he couldn't see all that was there. So he sent his ministers to bring back a full report.

The ministers couldn't see anything either, but the fear of being thought stupid or unfit for office had them go back to the emperor and rave about the beautiful garment that was (not) coming into view on the "magic" looms. Soon the whole town fell prey to the ruse. They talked of nothing but the wonderful cloth. The kingdom planned a big parade to celebrate the emperor's new clothes.

When the big day came, the Emperor strutted down the thoroughfare with his fawning entourage, pretending to be clad in regal garments, and thinking he was. Men of stature lined the street to acclaim his nonexistent finery as the crowd looked on approvingly. Suddenly, the high pitched voice of a child sounded above the crowd: "But he has nothing on at all!" The men of stature fell silent. The acclaim gave way to a murmur of agreement. The embarrassed emperor, however, felt compelled to continue the charade, parading down the street in his skivvies. His ministers followed behind him, carrying a train that didn't exist.

Time and again I've worn the emperor's illusionary clothes myself. I've taken other's beliefs and put them on and acted as if they were true for me, when in my gut I knew better. In my early twenties, I believed the theory that "thin is in." I shrunk to an incredible 85 lbs., hung on a 5'6" frame. If I gained a pound, I would write in my weekly weigh-in chart, "Lose it, Pig." Even as I was obsessing about being obese, my boss told me I'd have to run around in the shower just to get wet.

### Affirmation

**I am beautiful and everybody loves me, just the way I am. I rejoice in my uniqueness.**

In my thirties, I was a workout-aholic. My twins would say, "Mama, you're a Barbie!" And I was. Right down to the teased blond hair, too-tight clothes, and high-heeled pumps. Today I recognize those shoes for what they were; instruments of torture. And I have the injured feet to prove it.

What is behind the obsession with appearance in our society? The author Sark, in her book,

*Prosperity Pie – How to Relax About Money and Everything Else*, says the biggest problem is that people think they aren't enough. If we had more of this and less of that, then and only then would we be enough.

She suggests going on a hunt for our own inner treasures – wear a tutu, eat fruit naked, cavort in the grass, drink lemonade, walk barefoot, climb trees, listen to spiritual songs. "Be an emotional pioneer who takes tender, exquisite care of your very own soul," Sark says. "The more that each of us tends our own soul, the more the world will prosper."

## Walk On The Wild Side

- Paint your toenails blue, purple or iridescent colors
- Practice yoga or tai chi outdoors
- Hug a tree and feel its essence
- Visit a music store and play tunes you never heard before

- Browse a book store and sample all sorts of different topics and authors
- Go to a tall building downtown and ride the elevator up and down watching people

- Take a vacation by yourself. Make a point of talking to strangers and learning about their lives.

The underlying wisdom here is that we are not just flesh, blood, skin, and bones. We are souls that need to be tended, just as much as we are bodies that need to be fed and adorned. This is one of the hardest truths to grasp for ourselves; because our society assigns us our value based solely on how we look. The soul is unseen, and therefore its value is easy to discount. Yet if we neglect our inner selves, we dissolve into a bundle of desires, fears, and doubts, because the very nature of the body is temporary and therefore limited. As I came to grips with this truth, I was more and more able to drop the masks that kept me from connecting with others authentically. As I let go of the illusions that obscured my vision, I began to see my limitless nature.

None of us have to be duped by the emperor's weavers. Instead of being defined by the visions of the fashion industry, let us look to the beauty of our own soul.

Why not start today? Love yourself as you are and accept those around you. Affirm "I am loving and lovable. I love being me!" When you can calmly face your fears that you will be rejected, humiliated or shunned for being yourself, you will be flooded by the light of your own magnificence – your true self shining outward. You don't need the emperor's new clothes to impress.

# 6: Reuniting Families

*The problems that we experience in family relationships is usually dealt with in a context of self hatred and recrimination. "Shoulds" create guilt and despair. There is a better way.*

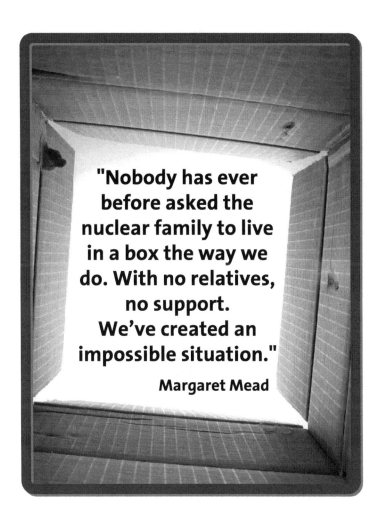

"Nobody has ever before asked the nuclear family to live in a box the way we do. With no relatives, no support.
We've created an impossible situation."

Margaret Mead

## See the Symptom;
## Treat the Cause

In my vocation, I see more than my share of children who come from backgrounds of abuse and neglect. I grieve each time I'm involved in a case where children are abandoned to hunger, or when they suffer harm at the hands of a caretaker who is under the influence of alcohol or drugs.

These are the kids who usually end up in foster homes, and involved with the courts. As often as not, case workers and judges blame substance abuse as the root cause. Very few people ask the deeper question: "Why are these parents using drugs in the first place?"

It's easy to treat the symptom, and ignore the cause. Like Nancy Reagan said: "Just say 'No'". This is the mentality that leads courts to remove children from their parents. Then they require the parents to get jobs, find better housing, or undergo substance abuse treatment before they can be reunited with their children.

If the parents were capable of doing these things, they would already be doing them! And so, many never do, and generations of kids grow up as wards of the court. Worse, they learn the same patterns of behavior, which they then pass on to the next generation. And so the cycle continues.

It's great to preach against drug abuse-- but, before anything can really shift, people need emergency first aid to treat the harm that is caused by their own negative self-image. Before a person is ever able to recognize the harmful consequences of drugs, they must find a better alternative. They must be able to look in the mirror and see someone they love. Only then does it make sense to say "No" to drugs. Otherwise, the need to self-medicate remains.

In truth, people who abuse drugs are often treating the pain of self rejection with the chemicals. Addictions come from low self-esteem. One counselor I met told me that he asks new patients to list ten things they like about themselves. Some patients can't identify more than two qualities before breaking down in tears. These are the cases in which parents pass the hatred and contempt they feel for themselves onto their children, creating generations of despair. Neglect of themselves translates into neglect of their children. This pattern has to stop.

In truth, people who abuse drugs and neglect their children have the same good desires for their children as anyone else. Instead of ordering these parents to stop taking drugs if they want to maintain their families, they need to start by learning positive affirmations. "I love and appreciate myself." "I am a good and loving parent."

For several years, I used marijuana to escape an unhappy marriage. This avenue of escape alienated me from my most important relationships, and cost me some wonderful opportunities to prosper in my business and personal life. One day, by chance, I discovered Louise L. Hay's book, *You Can Heal Your Life*. In it, I read:

"Self-approval and self-acceptance in the now are the main keys to positive changes in every area of our lives. Loving the self. . .begins with never ever criticizing ourselves for anything. Criticism locks us into the very pattern we are trying to move out of. Remember that you have been criticizing yourself for years, and it hasn't worked. Try approving of yourself and see what happens."

At first, these ideas made no sense to me. How was it possible to approve of myself when I was constantly confronted with the consequences of my own mistakes and failings? As I read the book with receptivity, however, I began the path of healing.

I soon learned that, when I really loved and accepted and APPROVED OF MYSELF exactly as I was, then everything in my life began to work. It was as if little miracles were everywhere. My health improved, I attracted more money, my relationships become much more fulfilling and I begin to express myself in creatively fulfilling ways. All of this seemed to happen without my even trying.

In *The Royal Tenenbaums*, Gene Hackman plays a dysfunctional father who decides after ten years' absence after his divorce to help restore his children's self-esteem. He teaches them all to hoot, holler, laugh and play. He takes his fearful son (Ben Stiller) and grandsons for a ride on the ledge of a dump truck. He gives of himself and restores his family.

People who indulge in self criticism never really enjoy anything. They are too busy reliving every failure in the never-ending saga of defeat that is their lives. And they never really change.

In my own experience, self-criticism never kept me from repeating an undesired behavior. Quite the opposite was true. It was only when I began affirming the behavior I wanted to adopt and refused to criticize myself, no matter what, that I began to make positive changes in my life.

For example, I used to be late for all of my court hearings. It's not that I didn't care about my appointments. I had an ugly, old alarm clock, rigged with a siren to scare me out of bed. Still I arrived late. Habitually. Each time, as it became clear that I was going to be tardy again, I drove to court with visions of the dire consequences that I feared would be in store. I was angry with myself, and very stressed out.

One day, I was two hours late for court driving at top speed. Again, I was imagining what I expected would be a smug opponent, an embarrassed client, and an angry judge. This time, I decided to affirm: "I am in the right place at the right time, doing the right thing."

Slowly and with hesitation, I began to speak. My heart was palpitating. My hands were shaking, and my palms were sweating. My words did not feel true. Still I refused to give in to the dread and lapse into self criticism. When I arrived, I found that the case had been postponed three hours! I was actually early for the trial. I met with my client. We reviewed the particulars, and went forward.

I continued repeating my affirmations and refusing to criticize myself and soon, I began to arrive on time for almost everything. The change was almost effortless, and its effects, remarkable. I threw out the old alarm clocks. Instead, each time I arrived for an appointment on time, I praised myself. Soon, the need for a siren alarm was replaced by a wakeful "me" who arose right on time each day to do the right thing, in the right place.

## Affirmation

> I get high on life. It is easy to make positive, healthy changes that benefit my family and me.

A side benefit of this practice was the insight I gained into the true cause of my chronic tardiness. At the time, I was a criminal defense lawyer, at my husband's insistence. I resented it. My lateness to court hearings was actually a passive way of expressing my resentment. Yet until I stopped criticizing myself, I was blind to the source of my behavior. Criticism blinds us, and binds us, to the very behavior we resist. Praise sets us free.

When we begin to treat ourselves right, our loved ones are the first ones to benefit. One self-help author I know says that children hear the word "no" from parents fifty times for every "yes". As we begin to heal ourselves, we will naturally reach out to heal our children with loving, affirmative messages. And it carries out from there. As a society we need to rethink methods that make parents of distressed families into villains and losers. Instead we need to support parents with messages of self-esteem and praise for their essential self-worth as a human being, and meet their failings with counseling, not condemnation.

Quite often, child protective agencies require parents to sign onto agreements that begin with an assumption that the parents are basically failures. What if agency agreements in such cases recognized the parents' desire to do the best they can for their children, and stated means of supporting their efforts, instead of a "to do" list of needed improvements. Would they not be more successful? I say they would.

It is a worthy experiment in any case. If all the money spent litigating child protective cases went to positive rehabilitation, there would be less need for funds to spend on incarceration. Who know? We might find the next generation to be more enlightened than ever before.

## Family Movies to Rent or Own

- ✓ *Royal Tenenbaums* - A dysfunctional father seeks to make things right before he dies.
- ✓ *The Nutty Professor* - The Klump family laugh their way through food and foibles.
- ✓ *Raising Arizona* - A cop and an ex-con steal a baby to make a family.

✓ *Dr. Doolittle* - A doctor discovers he can talk to animals to the delight of his children and woe of the medical community.

✓ *The Truman Show* - For everyone who wishes life would be perfect, here is one man who finds out truth and sensitivity mean far more than beautiful people and scenery.

✓ *To Kill a Mockingbird* - A small town lawyer risks income and reputation to take on a racially charged case because he believes in humanity.

✓ *Field of Dreams* -- A farmer builds a baseball diamond in a cornfield with the help of his wife and daughter, so he can summon back the ghosts of past players.

✓ *The Power of One* - A young man who becomes an orphan at age six grows up to become an advocate for the end to apartheid in South Africa.

✓ *Pay It Forward* - A young boy comes up with a plan that will truly change the world for the better, one person at a time.

# 7: Starve Your Negative Thoughts

*At one point in my life, it took me two hours to get ready for court.*
*I was always late, trying to make sure I looked "perfect." The trouble was, I missed out on the case because I wasn't there. Don't make the mistake of waiting until you're "perfect" to show up in life. Be there NOW!*

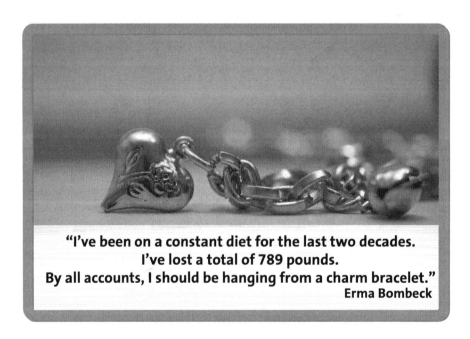

"I've been on a constant diet for the last two decades.
I've lost a total of 789 pounds.
By all accounts, I should be hanging from a charm bracelet."
Erma Bombeck

## A Diet Tip That Works

Why do people spend millions of dollars on diets, and then end up gaining back even more than when they started? I have a tip that will make you feel good and won't cost you a dime. Go on a diet from negative thoughts. You will lose weight, and gain self-esteem.

What you put your attention on increases, and what you turn your attention from, withers and dies. If you are continually telling yourself "Don't eat that!" your subconscious mind hears it as an instruction: "Eat that! Eat That. EAT THAT!" And eat it you will. If you are saying "I don't want to be fat." Your subconscious mind hears "...want to be fat." Why is this so? Because your thoughts flow in pictures, and when you call up a bad picture, it becomes an order to your subconscious mind.

If you want to be someone who is comfortable in their own skin, you need to begin from a standpoint of love and self acceptance based on the simple truth that you exist. This is a fact. It is not based on some recent achievement. If it were, then no one could ever do enough, because there are always things about us that need to improve. Criticism produces only negative changes. Praise produces positive good. I have seen this work in my own life, many times.

For example, when my husband and I separated, our son Alex's twelve year old life unraveled. From his point of view, his entire world had already become much harder when he changed from a private to a public school the previous fall, and he had to break into a new group of kids. His response was to turn to food for comfort, and he put on 25 lbs. The kids at his new school mocked him with cruel names, and denied him a seat on the bus. Alex is by nature sweet, and so it was not in him to fight back. He just came home, opened the refrigerator and began stuffing more food into his mouth. As a mother, I felt powerless to soothe his pain. Since I have a black belt in karate, I could easily have knocked off a few of his tormenters. Believe me; I wanted to do just that! I would have felt better, but it wouldn't help Alex win his own battles.

At night, when my children were asleep, I used go into their rooms and kiss them. One night, I went into my son's room, and watched him as he slept. What I saw broke my heart. There was so much fat on his face, I could hardly see the handsome young man underneath. I thought, "My beautiful boy is trapped in a prison of fat. No one can even see the child I know." I knew that if he stayed in that place, he was in for decades of unhappiness.

As I watched Alex in his sleep, I decided to find a way to help him. I knew from past experience helping others to lose weight that fat indicates a need for protection. Alex's life was in flux over our breakup, and the unkind remarks of the kids at school hurt him. He was eating emotionally, to ease his pain.

I could see that Alex believed that he needed to lose weight in order to become someone his peers would like. He thought that weight loss would change who he was as a person, yet he couldn't stop eating, so he felt even worse about himself. Forcing Alex to control his eating, or deny himself the comfort of food, would only lead him to feel more grief, and more gluttony. If he was going to do something that really worked, I knew I would have to help Alex in a positive way.

The next morning, I approached my son. I assured him that, with or without the extra weight, he was already good enough the way he was. I recalled the day he was born, and I told him about the extraordinary qualities I had seen in his character in those first moments of his life. I said, "Alex, there is nothing you need to change. I was there when you were born. I know who you are. You are a wonderful person. If you would find it convenient to lose weight, I will help you, son. But you need to understand that you are good enough as you are, right now." Alex thoughtfully responded that he would like to lose the weight.

Diets don't work if they seem like punishment, so I did not remove the junk food from our house. I never counted Alex's calories. I never told him what not to eat, and I never told him to weigh himself. Instead, I made up a system of "Do's" not "Don'ts." I call it the "Five Alive" plan.

## Five Alive Plan

1. Eat *five* fruits or veggies each day

2. Drink *five* glasses of water each day

3. Exercise at least 30 minutes, *five* times a week

4. Think of *five* things you're grateful for before bedtime each night

5. Praise yourself lavishly each time you fulfill one of these commitments, and refuse to criticize yourself when you don't.

There is nothing scientific about it. The first rule was that Alex had to eat five fruits or vegetables every day. My theory was that if he was busy eating good foods, he might not have room left for the high calorie snacks. The second rule was that he had to drink five glasses of water each day. The third rule was that we had to exercise every day.

The genius of the plan (if I may commend myself) was the third rule. I gave Alex my Self: Whatever workout he chose, I agreed to do it with him. Alas! He picked street hockey and soccer. I wasn't much good at either sport, but I followed along.

Sometimes we would walk around the block or exercise at a gym. The point is I never punished Alex for eating. I never made him stand on a scale for inspection. I just allowed him to feel that his choice of exercise was the most fun thing we both could be doing with our day.

Three months later, Alex got on a scale at the doctor's office and let out a holler, "Mom, I lost 30 pounds!" That fall, things changed with the kids at school. Alex found friends who shared his interest in exercise. This allowed me to return to my interest in karate.

Alex went on to become the captain of his high school swim team. After high school, he earned a four-year tuition scholarship at the University of Michigan. Today, he has a 5'10", 180 lb. body, and he is truly a beautiful young man.

## Affirmation

*I love and accept myself, exactly as I am right now. I have a slender, healthy body that is perfect for me in this lifetime.*

The same principle that worked for Alex can work for you. Be willing to see the beauty that is inside you. Say, "I love you" to yourself when you look at yourself in the mirror. Love yourself. Accept who you are. Refuse to criticize yourself, no matter what. Tell yourself: "I have the perfect body for me in this lifetime." Maybe you have marvelous, soft skin. Maybe you have pretty eyes. Whatever your particular advantages, realize that you are a magnificent Being of

Light. As you believe, you will achieve.

I can hear you right now. You are saying, "But I hate my skin tone!" or "I am so fat I can't stand to look at myself with the lights on!" Maybe you've tried everything short of stomach shrinking surgery. But thoughts about weight – or any addictive behavior – are only thoughts, and a thought can be changed.

Start by understanding the truth about yourself: You are a manifestation of the divine life. Therefore, you are worthy of love just as you are. If you decide it would be convenient for you to lose weight, then do so, but release the need to punish yourself with a strict diet. Try the "Five Alive" plan, or some other sensible eating strategy, for yourself. Remember, you deserve to radiate to the world at your ideal weight. Find a friend who will exercise with you. It is being strong to ask for help when you need it. Instead of meeting over meals why not meet friends at the park for a walk and talk? You don't have a friend? Become your own friend. Start there, and you will attract friends. It all starts with loving yourself, exactly as you are, right now. Try it, and you will get where you want to go.

# 8: Surviving Divorce

*On the day of my own divorce, I sat in court and listened to a woman arguing with her lawyer. The courtroom was empty, and her case was delayed. She was clearly not accustomed to the pressure of financial responsibility, she was afraid for her future, and so she was resentful about her attorney's fees. At one point, she exclaimed, "I don't care! If you can't make the divorce final today, I'm not paying you." Without a word, her lawyer got up and walked out of the courtroom, leaving her alone in stunned silence. I wanted to comfort her, but she was not my client. Not to mention that I was going through the same process at that moment myself...*

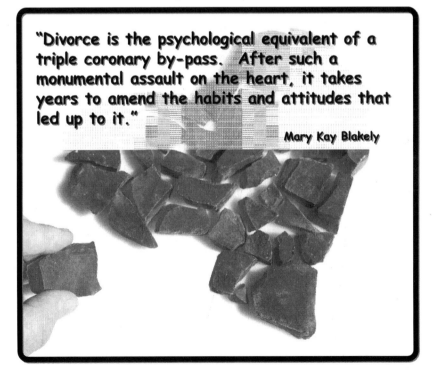

"Divorce is the psychological equivalent of a triple coronary by-pass. After such a monumental assault on the heart, it takes years to amend the habits and attitudes that led up to it."

Mary Kay Blakely

## Taking Your Break-up to Breakthrough

The challenges faced by couples today are very potent, and it's no surprise that half of all marriages in America are ending up in divorce. When you are going through it, it's easy to forget that you are not alone; but the statistic is true, and it has been true in America for most of our lives. To me, it is a wonder that so many couples stay together as long as they do! That said, no matter how you feel; lonely, angry, depressed (and you will wrestle with all these feelings), you must be mindful of your children. In meeting their needs, you often meet your Self.

In the last twenty years, I have seen hundreds of couples end their marriages. I have been through the process myself. This is what I discovered: Divorce can be one of the most traumatic events of your life. That's not usually avoidable. Yet it can also be a doorway to growth, healing, and spiritual reconstruction. The difference lies in how you decide to view the experience. That is where you can claim your power.

Divorce is almost never conflict free, but if you keep your focus on your responsibilities, and try to be fair to everyone involved, the adjustment can be managed.

A breakup brings negative feelings like clouds and wind brings rain. In the heat of a breakup, you will probably spend a fair amount of your time being just plain angry. You will be mad at your spouse. You will be mad at yourself. You will feel guilty. You will feel "I just got screwed." You may experience the gnaw of jealousy. That's all par for the course. How you decide to handle these feelings is up to you, and that is what makes all the difference.

When you are angry with someone close to you, it's natural to want to express it to your closest friends, and to the family that knows you both. Everybody needs a listening ear. You may want to tell your kids all about the bad qualities of your soon-to-be-ex. Don't do it.

Parents are like gods to their children, and they need to keep both of you in their hearts. They are watching everything you do, and your response to this divorce will teach them more about love relationships than anything you could every say. The way you carry yourself will either reinforce their own self image, or tear down their hopes for a happy life. It's important to remember that no matter how you feel, you are the adult, not the child. Don't deprive them of their childhood by relying on them to shepherd your own inner child.

The woman you are divorcing is their mother. If you criticize her, you are creating confusion. That man you are talking about is their father. If you trash him as worthless, you are effectively making your child fatherless.

Remember, it was you who chose that person to be a parent for your children. Now that you are splitting up, they are going through a divorce too. Your children are not judges. You have no right to use them to validate your disappointment about your spouse, at the expense of their right to love and respect the woman and the man who brought them into this world. Do not ask them to try your case and decide who is "right" and who is "wrong." If you do, they are just as likely to take the blame themselves rather than condemn either one of you. You don't want that. Take responsibility for yourself, and leave your partner to God and to the court.

Sure, you can "win" the battle for their hearts and minds in the short term. But in the long term, this strategy will backfire. No won wins a war in which the battleground is your own home and close relationships. Your animosities will force your friends and family to take sides. "His and her" vindictive accusations and defensive recriminations will increase the legal fees you both incur; and face it; a marriage is like a business. When it dissolves, there are assets to be divided. Any money spent on lawyers is just that much less that goes to either of you from the marital estate.

Don't get me wrong. Good legal representation is an important component of a rehabilitative divorce, but going to divorce court to gain wealth is like going to war to get someone else's gold. Even if you win, you spend so much more on the fight than you get in booty that it's just not worth the cost. If you end up in separate waiting rooms at the mediation to avoid an outright confrontation in front of other clients you have embarrassed yourself. Meanwhile, the things that are truly precious are slipping through your fingers.

Do you want your children's loyalty after the divorce? Show them love during the divorce. That doesn't mean getting into a contest with your spouse to see who has more money to spend on shiny things. It means giving your Self. It means giving them your time; taking them places they enjoy, like an aircraft show or a skating exhibition. It can mean staying home together and making a pizza from scratch. It means giving them the freedom to love *both* their parents, without guilt. The most important part of the picture is YOU.... together with your child. The time and place are just background.

Of course, you need to vent your feelings about your spouse. So talk it out with a friend or therapist. When your children are visiting the other spouse, plan something fun to do yourself so you don't feel lonely or jealous. These feelings are just thoughts, and thoughts can be changed. Realize that no one can ever replace you in your child's life.

If you are able to stop fighting, or using the children as pawns on the chessboard, you will make the separation process smoother. As a result, your legal costs will decrease and you will help bring about your own recovery. The war is over. Stop fighting.

When I got divorced, it was I who initiated it. I had reasons. If I had allowed myself to focus on my reasons, instead of my responsibilities, I could have spiraled into a fury of rage and vengeance. Instead, I chose love. Why? I remembered the law of karma: What we send out comes back. What did I want coming back to me? I wanted good; and so I chose to remember that the man I was divorcing was the same man that I had once deeply loved. And that's how I think of him to this day.

Did I make this choice because I am so enlightened? It depends upon what you call "enlightened." I simply remembered my own parents' bitter divorce and the impact it had on me. I decided to handle mine differently.

When you realize that your marriage is over, you will want to blame someone for the lost time, and all the ways your needs have been disappointed. If you choose to blame your spouse, you make yourself a victim, and victims have no power. The truth is it takes two to make or break any marriage.

Or you may begin to excoriate yourself for the fact that you chose to marry this person in the first place. This speculation is unfair to you and to your ex to be, and the exercise is destructive to you both. Perhaps the negative has overwhelmed the positive, and so it's best to divorce. But beating yourself up for what you now see as a bad decision is just another way of blocking the truth of your situation, so you won't see it. There were good reasons you fell in love with and chose to marry this person. Be willing to sit with a glass of muddy water until it settles and becomes clear. The lessons that await you will then become apparent.

The simple truth is that everyone does the best they can with the knowledge, information, and awareness they have. If you could have done better, you would have done better. Every moment of your life is valid and precious, and your relationships do not end with divorce; they only change. Keep the good memories. Learn from the past. Treat this knowledge as a gift and move on.

## Master Yourself and Look Ahead. That's Where You're Going!

Abraham Lincoln once said "It is best to ride a horse in the direction it's going." Similarly, when going through a divorce you do not want to keep looking backward. Divorce always brings loss before it brings gain. Anger is a natural phase in the process of adjustment to great loss. Pain is part of the process. You need to release these feelings. If you suppress anger, the pain doesn't go away. It stays stuck in your body and can cause internal problems: headaches, digestive problems, high blood pressure, heart disease, anxiety and depression. According to Swami Sivananda:

A terrible fit of anger shatters the physical nervous system. It produces a lasting impression on the inner astral body. Although the effects of a fit of anger may seem to subside in a short time, the vibration or wave continues to exist for days in the astral body. A slight unpleasant feeling that lasts in the mind for five minutes may produce a deep inflammation of the astral body. It may take several weeks or months even for this ulcer to heal.

I believe there are only two emotions; love and fear. Anger is a manifestation of fear, and trying to "stuff it" or shame yourself out of having it is unhealthy, and unwise. Let your feelings pass

**57**

through you, like the shadow of a bird overhead. They are just feelings; they're not you.

Are you angry that the time you spent with your spouse has caused you to lose time that you could have spent on other relationships? As time passes, and you get some perspective, that will change. Learn to trust that you are in the right place at the right time, doing the right thing. Every moment you spent with your spouse helped you become the person that you are today. Now, you can channel your energies it into new relationships. Begin with yourself. Expect more of yourself. You will get more back.

Meanwhile, you're "pissed", and there is nothing wrong with that unless you fail to release it. Some people like to pound a "heavy bag" with a plastic bat (the bag used by boxers and students of the martial arts)--or if you're out of shape, go punch a pillow or start an exercise program. Exercise is a tremendous de-stressor. I had a friend who lost 35 lbs. in 90 days. How? He spent an hour a day on a treadmill. "It helps me think," he said. And remember, when you exercise you increase the number of endorphins in your brain, those wonderful chemicals that block pain and lift your spirits.

Remember my suggestion at the end of Chapter 3? Write that angry letter to your spouse. Don't hold back. Tell him exactly what he has done to disappoint you. Recite every hurt he has inflicted on you. Call him every pejorative name that describes him. When you are finished, fold up the letter and write, "What I really want from you is your love and approval."

Now, take the letter, read it to yourself, and tell yourself the truth: "It doesn't matter if he ever understands what I have said here. I understand myself. From this moment, I am free". Now, tear it to pieces and burn it.

You will be amazed at how much satisfaction this exercise brings. By burning the letter, you enter the point of power and assume control of your own emotions.

Note: None of these suggestions involve expressing anger to your spouse. For example, if you punch your spouse instead of a pillow, you go to jail. If you send that letter, you will escalate the battle and excite the qualities in your spouse that led to the divorce in the first place. That puts you in a more precarious legal position, because the person with the most clarity has the strategic advantage in any lawsuit. Listen to your heart. Keep your head, and you will win respect.

Although it will take time, the ultimate goal here is to reach the point where you believe: "I am 100% responsible for everything that happens in my life." Make this truth your own, and you are on the path to real power.

Let's take an example: In our society, men still tend to have higher incomes than women, and women usually have a higher risk to their lifestyle in a divorce. Most women are daunted at the financial consequences of their breakup because they are asked to go from a state of participation in their husband's income, to a "fixed" income. Most women never ask themselves: Who "fixes" income? The contributor or the recipient? Obviously, the recipient does. The recipient has the power to create new streams of income and a new life.

J. K. Rowling, a divorced mother, wrote her first Harry Potter novel on a shoestring, and the series has become one of the best-read children's books of the last decade. She chose to take personal responsibility for her life and decided she would make it, no matter what. If you are open and receptive to the abundance that is in the world, you can clear the way for new avenues of income and earn as much money as you want to receive.

## TRUST THE PROCESS

It's natural to ask: "Why is this happening to me?" Emmanuel, a spiritual teacher, says: "See painful circumstances as lessons, not as retribution. You have come to traverse a wide terrain of experience in order to verify where truth lies, and where your distortion is in that terrain. However far afield life seems to take you, this trip is necessary. You will then be able to return to your home center, your soul self, refreshed and wiser."

Go to the mirror. Look at your own face. Look into your eyes, and see the person staring back at you. There is a human being of tremendous value. This is not true because you realize it. It is an absolute. You can anchor yourself to that. So do it. Say: "I love and appreciate you just the way you are, right now." Does this feel uncomfortable? Say it anyway, and just allow yourself to notice the things that come up. You may find that you have been very hard on yourself and this is a difficult thing to do. Don't criticize yourself; just notice. And continue speaking loving words to yourself, every time you look into the mirror.

If you learn the lessons and are willing to change, your divorce can be a catalyst to an extraordinary life. Allow your break-up to become a breakthrough that takes you to a higher level.

## Affirmation:

I love myself.
I can love again.
I am wonderful,
whole, and complete,
just as I am.

## Toss A Goddess Party!

Acknowledge the transition as you move from being married to single. Invite your girlfriends to join you for a monthly party that celebrates the whole wide world of womanhood.

- ✓ Make pretty invitations with glitter, ribbons, calligraphy and fancy paper.
- ✓ Invite women from different ages, countries, and occupations.
- ✓ Ask everyone to bring a dish and a beverage. It's no fun spending all your time cooking.
- ✓ Recite a favorite poem. Each person shares a treasure.
- ✓ Acknowledge the gifts that came from your marriage (e.g., children, adventures, experiences) and state your positive intentions for the future.
- ✓ Enjoy the love and support of your sisters in spirit.

# 9: The Hero In You

*"I need a hero!  I'm holding out for a hero 'til the end of the night."* **Sings Bonnie Raitt. Everybody wants a hero to come from the outside, break into their life and solve their problems. The happiest among us find that hero waiting in a place closer than you might expect.**

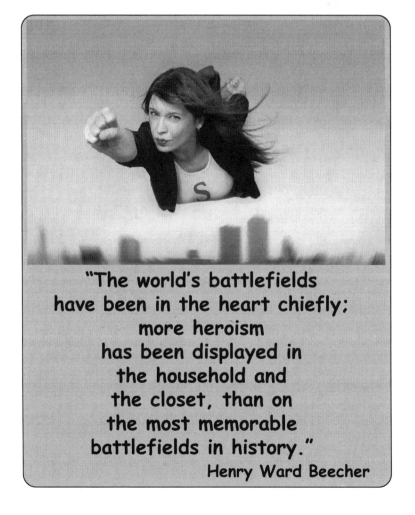

"The world's battlefields
have been in the heart chiefly;
more heroism
has been displayed in
the household and
the closet, than on
the most memorable
battlefields in history."
Henry Ward Beecher

## What Makes a Hero?

In the 1997 movie *Liar, Liar*, actor Jim Carrey plays "Fletcher Reed", a scalawag lawyer whose son's magical birthday wish renders him physically unable to lie for 24 hours. Desperate to avoid a trial he cannot conduct with honesty, he goes into the restroom and begins beating himself up. An older man comes in and watches him in horror. "What are you doing?" he asks. Fletcher Reed responds, "Can't you see? I'm kicking my ass!"

How many of us spend days, months, and years kicking the only one who really has the power to allow us to become what we were meant to be? Somewhere we learned that if we think highly of ourselves, we would get a swelled head. When someone compliments us, we shrug it off: "It was nothing, really." We play ourselves down and look for inspiration outside ourselves. This wrong-headed view of humility is self destructive and unwise.

***Most people never realize that the only one who can inspire us to be what we were meant to be is the hero inside.***

In this, the Masters agree: Heroic character springs from an appreciation of one's own true value. Classic integrity is firmly rooted in Self-respect. This, of course, differs from mere arrogance. Arrogance and vanity are only fear, and a far cry from true self-respect.

In *Records of the Grand Historian*, ancient Chinese chronicler Si Ma Qian describes the oriental concept of integrity:

*He will honor his words; he will definitely carry out his actions. What he promises he will fulfill. He does not care for his bodily self, putting his life and death aside to come forward for another's troubled besiegement. He does not boast about his ability, or shamelessly extol his own virtues.*

True integrity shows a quiet reluctance to trumpet one's own virtues; but it is not a blindness to the fact that they are there.

What is the difference between appreciating one's own magnificence and mere arrogance? *A Course in Miracles* describes the chasm that lies between "grandiosity," which is rooted in fear, and true grandeur, which is the stuff of nobility. Grandiosity is a fool's gold, a glaze to cover underlying despair. Grandeur is an emanation of the natural light that is all around and within us.

Les Brown is one of the most sought after motivational speakers in the world. He was born in poverty. As a child, his teachers wrote him off as "retarded." During his life he has contended with cancer and divorce. He attributes his staying power to a rock-solid belief in himself, explaining: "You cannot take strength from the good parts of yourself that you don't know are there."

Les is right. Every one of us has a hero within who can uplift us when we are down. Unless we are willing to recognize this, however, our inner hero cannot help us.

Joaquim Pereira is not a celebrity. He is not an author. He is not glamorous or famous or wealthy. He is a 66 year old farmer who lives in the village of Cosmorama, Brazil. On February 8, 2007, his eight-year-old grandson, Matheus, was playing with friends in a creek bed when a fifteen foot anaconda attacked him. The friends went to get help, and the older man went down into a ravine to find the largest species of serpent on this planet wrapped around his head. The man grabbed the snake with his hands, but the monster was too strong to dislodge. "When I saw the snake wrapped around my grandson's neck, I thought it was going to kill him," Joaquim Pereira told the Agencia Estado news service. "It was agonizing, I pulled it from one side, but it would come back on the other."

Most people would have gone for help at that point, but Pereira did not have time to go looking for a hero. He did not have the luxury of throwing up his hands because he was "just too old for that sort of thing." He had to do what he had to do. He grabbed a machete, and spent 45 minutes hacking on the creature until finally, he killed it.

When he was done, the child had a gaping wound where the snake had bit him, but the serpent was dead and Joaquim Pereira had saved his grandchild. Viva Pereira! And Viva! To the hero within us all!

> ## Affirmation:
>
> **I am a magnificent child of God, and I rejoice in my uniqueness. I am a limitless being accepting from a limitless source in a limitless way.**
>
> **I love being me!**

It takes just as much courage to leave the coil of a failed marriage, and like Pereira's grandson, we don't escape unscarred. I've known clients who walked away with nothing but their children and the clothes on their back to escape a life of physical abuse. Heroically, they went on to make a new life for themselves and their children, despite the challenges they faced.

I knew a public relations woman who was stricken with kidney disease. In ten years of renal dialysis, she saw that many kidney patients were too impoverished to buy medicine. She organized a fundraiser to help buy necessities for low-income renal patients. This woman is a hero, and now she walks tall with her brother's kidney.

My former husband joined the army at 15 so that he could send a weekly check to his mother. She never went on welfare. He is a hero, although he cannot see it. By refusing to acknowledge himself for his loving sacrifice, he is failing to satisfy the vital need we all have for recognition.

His daughter, Toi, had a similar experience. She was left by her mother when she was 17 years old. Nevertheless, she raised her two younger sisters by working as a waitress, and made sure both girls finished high school and attended college. After their needs were met, Toi enrolled in college herself. Toi is a hero, no doubt, even though some people look at her and only see a waitress.

Everyone you meet has the qualities of a hero just under the surface. Every one of us has overcome challenging odds at some point in our lives. In everyone's life, there is something to admire—a story that would bring tears to your eyes, if you took the time to hear it. How many heroes do you know?

Where do you fit on your own list? Have you listened to your own story? Before you go to sleep each night, recite five things you accomplished that day; whether it is smiling at a clerk in the store, working out, or reading a book that gave you an insight.

The first challenge we encounter is our own low self-esteem. Criticism breaks us down, and praise builds us up. Be willing to praise yourself for what you have accomplished, and your list of accomplishments will grow. Praise yourself for big things and small! Don't compare yourself to others. Your journey is to discover what makes you great. When you do, your inner light will shine for one and all.

Marianne Williamson puts it brilliantly: "Your playing small doesn't serve the world. There's nothing enlightened about shrinking so that other people won't feel insecure around you. We are all meant to shine, as children do." Don't forget, you survived 40 million sperm just to show up. You were born a conqueror!

## Identify the Real You

Listen to your inner child. Look in the mirror and ask, "How can I make YOU happy today?" Do whatever your child suggests; maybe that means actually playing on a swing set, coloring, or skipping down the sidewalk. Maybe you need to go pull some weeds. The options are all yours.

As you honor the inner You, the outer You will begin to shine, as the hero within you already does.

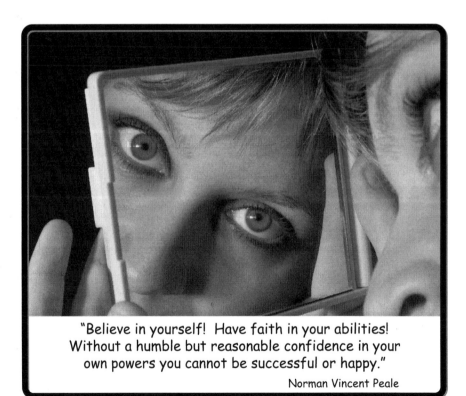

"Believe in yourself! Have faith in your abilities!
Without a humble but reasonable confidence in your
own powers you cannot be successful or happy."

Norman Vincent Peale

# 10: The Magic of Mistakes

*The only way for a person to fail is by quitting. We cannot fail, as long as we are working to reach our goals, finding new ways to turn our dreams into reality, and learning from our mistakes.*

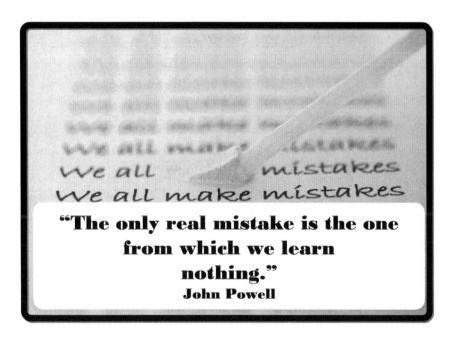

"The only real mistake is the one from which we learn nothing."
John Powell

## Learn, and Live!

A few years ago, an experienced snowboarder attended our Toastmaster's Club and showed us how it's done. It was easy, going through our paces in the conference room. My technique was perfect! The next thing I knew, I was in Colorado.

I have done aerobics for years. I have a black belt in karate. I can *do* anything if I really work at it. Nevertheless, I am not naturally athletic. Things don't just come to me. So here I was, staring down a snowy slope. I was great in practice, but when it came to actually doing the deed, that was quite a different matter! The thought of snowboarding down a mountain filled me with fear. In fact, that's exactly why I did it, because I felt so scared. How crazy is that?

Jim Rohn once said, "When the end comes, let it find you climbing up a *new* mountain, not sliding down an old one." Well, that was my goal. But as it turned out, I spent most of the day sliding down a new mountain!

I am sure I fell several dozen times, and the mountainside was dotted with knee and backside prints from my soaked blue jeans. At the end of the day, it seemed that every square inch of my body was bruised except my abdomen and my face. Nonetheless, I went out there and tried. In trying, I accomplished what I had set out to do: I conquered my fear, and made one more step on the path to self mastery.

Next time, I might even make it down the mountain in an upright position. Maybe I won't; or maybe it won't be until the time after that. It doesn't matter, because I've learned that I'm going to face some failures in life. I'm going to make mistakes along the way. I've also learned that the only real mistake, is giving up.

Thomas Edison was a man who knew about failure. He was a brilliant inventor, yet as a child he was called addled and was taken out of school after just 3 months. He was home schooled by his mother, and read and studied on his own. For most of his adult life, he was totally deaf.

In creating the electric light bulb, Edison failed ten thousand times before he finally succeeded. Ten thousand times! When is the last time any of us have persisted that long in any endeavor? How many of us give up after ten tries, or twenty, or fifty, or even a hundred? People around us say, "Don't worry, you did the best you could." But that wasn't good enough for Thomas Edison. When people chided him for his failure, he said, "I didn't fail. I just found 10,000 ways that didn't work."

Napoleon Hill is the author of the world famous book, *Think and Grow Rich*. He helped thousands of people to become millionaires. Despite this outstanding accomplishment, he himself did not become a millionaire until he was in his 80's. What kept him going, through disappointment after disappointment, failure after failure? He lived by the words of his mentor, Andrew Carnegie, that "Every failure carries with it the seeds of an equivalent or greater success." Hill found the magic in his mistakes, and kept pursuing his chief definite aim until he finally succeeded.

A more recent example is seen in the life of Chris Gardner, author of the best selling autobiography, "The Long Road to Happyness". Published by HarperCollins in 2006, Mr. Gardner relates a story of an abusive father and a "here today, gone tomorrow" mother who nevertheless taught him that he was responsible for his own success in life. The story that unfolds in the book tells of a single father who went from walking the streets homeless, to a millionaire many times over. Now his story of pain and challenge has become a book and a movie!

In a recent interview, Chris reflects:

"The first things kids want to know is how much money I make. For them, that's a validating question because it means: "Why should I listen to you?" My answer is always the same. If I were in the NBA, I might not be making as much as Shaq, but I wouldn't be on the bench, either. I tell them forget about money; money is the least significant aspect of wealth. It's more important to do something that makes you happy. Why do teachers teach? They've got passion for it. They do it to see the light come on in their kids' eyes."

Everyone who tries to accomplish anything in life experiences failure. In fact, the more often you try, the more often you fail. That is why Thomas J. Watson, founder of IBM, said the best way to succeed is to double your rate of failure.

Chris Gardner tried and failed and tried and failed, until one day he SUCCEEDED and became the powerful and influential man whom we see depicted by Will Smith in the inspiring movie *The Pursuit of Happyness*. The difference between average people and men like Chris Gardner is the ability to get back up after being knocked down; to learn from mistakes, and to move in a better direction. Remember; you only have to get back up one more time than you fall.

I was sixteen years old when I first tried to get a job. Day after day I tried at dozens of places, but the problem was the same: I needed a job to get experience, and I needed experience to get a job. Finally, I picked a particular restaurant I liked to apply for a job as a hostess. I went back, week after week, to fill out an application, until they finally got tired of seeing me come in, and hired me.

Throughout my life, I have learned that persistence and the refusal to accept failure, has enabled me to achieve successes I never thought possible. There is nothing more powerful than a made up mind!

After that snowboarding adventure, it hurt to sit down for awhile, but my bruises did not discourage me. I knew that it was just a little spilled milk, and I still had the cow.

How about you? What are your fields of interest and desire? Is it a new job, or a promotion? Do you want to learn a new sport, or master a new skill? Do you want to become an accomplished speaker, or do you want to help people overcome physical challenges? Whatever your dream is, write it down, break it up into written steps, and achieve them, one by one until you reach your goal.

Failure is just one kind of experience in an active life. It does not define who we are. There is magic in every mistake that you make, and if you are willing to see the lesson, your mistakes will teach you so much! Every mistake is a potential stepping stone to success, if you allow it to be. The journey of a thousand miles begins with the first step, and there may be many steps on your path, before you reach your goal.

If the greatest inventor of our time had to fail 10,000 times before he succeeded, what makes you think you ought to win on the first try? Lighten up. Love yourself, celebrate yourself, enjoy the magic of your mistakes, and never, ever, ever give up.

## How to Learn From Your Mistakes

1.  ***The next time you fail, refuse to criticize yourself, no matter what.***

There is a big difference between acknowledging your mistake and condemning yourself for making it. The next time you make a mistake, call it for what it is. Say: "What a wonderful opportunity for me to learn and grow!" Think about what you learned from the situation, and praise yourself for being wise enough to see it. Realize that you are a winner when you learn to fail forward.

*Affirmation:*
*I am willing to see the magic in my mistakes!*
*I see myself with compassion and love, and I accept all the parts of me.*
*All is well in my world.*

2. ***Examine your beliefs, to make sure that they are your partners in success.***

Ask:

What do I believe about myself?
Will I accept this as truth?

What do I believe about my future?
Will I accept this as truth?

What do I believe about my opportunities?
Will I accept this as the truth?

Write down what you believe, and then determine whether this is a positive, emotionally healthy belief. If it isn't, change your belief to one that supports you.  Your life is a made-up story anyway. Write one with a happy ending!

# 11: The Message From the Mess

*Recently, I was listening to a taped lecture by Les Brown, a world-renowned motivational speaker. He said that the reason inspiring others became his focus in life was because of his personal doubts about his own self-worth. As he said, "It's a message from my mess." What a great point! There is nothing we are more qualified to speak on, than the things that have most challenged us.*

*"Our doubts are traitors. They make us lose the good we oft might win, by failing to attempt."*

**William Shakespeare**

## Freedom From Fear

My life has been an abundance of good; my blessings, too many to number. Why, then, have I not had perfect joy all my days? Certainly, there have been hard times; but no ship comes to port without a storm or two. If I am fair, I must not blame the wind and waves. If I am just, I must admit that the main obstacle to my own happiness has always been my own FEAR.

I was raised by fearful parents who taught me to always play it safe. That is not to say I was always a scared little mouse! I have had my moments of courage, and they always carried a reward. As a young adult, I married a man whose ethnic background was different from my own. I made that choice because of the respect and love I had for him, not to offend my family. Nevertheless, my family ostracized me. Even though the marriage ended twenty-three years later, it was a fruitful choice for me. Bud and I have two lovely children who have brought great joy to our lives.

Fear has been the gatekeeper on the bridge between my present circumstances and the successes of which I dreamed. Sadly, I have not always paid the toll:

As a younger woman, I feared that I was not worthy to merit my husband's love if I stood my ground; and so I gave in to him until there was almost nothing left of me to yield. One day, I realized that I had no choice but to either separate from him entirely, or become simply an appendage to his ego. And so, after 23 years together, that marriage failed. The very thing I'd feared became my choice.

After our divorce, there was my fear waiting to greet me, like a bully in the schoolyard after the final bell.

How was I going to manage all the bills and raise the kids by myself? I had other fears as well: Fear of failure; a fear of looking foolish; a fear of not being good enough; a fear of not meriting love. Like sentinels around my bed, these fears kept watch with me through many a sleepless night.

Then there was the loneliness. Because of my fears, I kept silent; and so I believed that I was the only one who had to contend with such fears. I pretended that all was well, not only for the sake of my pride but primarily to shield my children from very real financial concerns that I felt they should not have to worry about. Consequently, I lost opportunities to form wholesome relationships with other people who could have identified with me, and whom I could have helped in turn.

As Franklin Delano Roosevelt said, "We have nothing to fear but fear itself." And so, I also feared that I would never get past these and other, like fears. Looking back, my fears created a potent barrier to prosperity and my happiness in my life. As Robert Kiyosaki's "rich dad" said, in *Retire Young, Retire Rich*:

> **It is your fear that makes you a prisoner. It is your fear that locks you in your own cell, a prison that does not let the abundance of God in.**

The root of all these fears is a false belief that we are helpless; unable to determine what kind of life we will have. The truth is that we create our lives with our beliefs. At a week-long training in 1999 based on Louise Hay's book, *You Can Heal Your Life*, I learned for the first time to tap into the power of my thoughts to create my own experience. It was then that the fears took their leave (or should I say, I felt the fears and did it anyway), the barriers to joy began to fall away, and my life changed forever.

I have never looked back since. To everyone out there who experiences fear as I have, and still do, my message is this: The human brain is the most sophisticated, complex, powerful computer in the world. Our minds are powerful instruments of creation which give form to the objects of our attention. Whether we go to the moon, or to an asylum for the mentally ill, our destiny is a function of our wonderful minds! In this way, our own thoughts create our reality. Whatever we give our attention to increases. Whatever we believe about ourselves comes true for us. That is why it is so important to focus on what we want, not what we don't want!

The question is, "What are you doing to harness this awesome gift?" Do you sit passively in front of a television, allowing the thoughts of others to determine your beliefs, your knowledge, your opinions; even your mood? Or do you actively give your attention to creating the life you really want? The power is yours. Therefore, the choice and the responsibility are also yours. Claim your power and resolve never to be a victim again.

When my daughter was 17, she was a very intelligent young lady; and yet it seemed that we had been fighting since the day she was born. I objected to her messy room, to her hygiene, to the amount of time she spent on the telephone, and so forth. Her failings were my focus.

In her junior year, she dropped out of high school and went to live with her father. "Where did I go wrong?" I lamented. On reflection, I realized that my fear that my daughter would turn out badly was creating the result I was getting. Right then I determined to affirm what I DID want for Lexie. Instead of trying to control her, I decided to establish a ritual to discipline my thoughts about her. Every night, I lit a candle and read aloud from a little slip of paper, without variation: "I am so happy and grateful that my daughter is a successful, top-notch student with high self-esteem, and positive goals, which she is highly motivated to achieve. Her life is filled with joy and love." Then I closed my eyes and visualized her as the young woman I knew she was capable of being.

At first, there was no change. Her father kept calling to report the latest "crazy" thing she was doing. I would say, "I don't even want to hear it. I am focusing on the Alexis I know she is capable of being." When she came to my house and did things that set me off, I kept my focus on the vision I had of her, and responded accordingly.

Within a few months of beginning this ritual, my daughter moved back home. She began an accelerated program, and finished high school. Her room, which used to be disorderly, became spotless; her drawers, full of neatly folded clothes. In her entire life, her room never looked like this! On top of her dresser was a list of goals, neatly itemized with target completion dates. It was an absolute miracle! All this happened without any suggestions from me.

*Affirmation:*

*I release the need to be fearful. I now welcome an abundance of peace, love, joy, and prosperity into my life.*

Since those first days, I have experienced many blessings by focusing on what I wanted, instead of what I did NOT want. As Wayne Dyer once said, "I'll see it when I believe it." So believe it! And you will see.

## The Power of a Thought

**Our thoughts are powerful, for they have the power of creation. Look what we have created in the economy by focusing on our fears, and visualizing the worst. I believe it's high time to change that reality, and I have a few suggestions:**

- Avoid excessively watching the news. The news is structured to keep you scared, continuing the "chain of pain," as Dr. Christianne Northrup calls it.

- Refuse to focus on hypothetical disasters, or negative "what if's." When fear thoughts come up, realize they are trying to protect you. Thank them for sharing, then let them go.

- Start your own daily routine for visualizing what you do want: a flourishing economy, abundant health, prosperity, a happy family. Think from your goals, not of them. Act "as if" they have already been realized.

- Have an "attitude of gratitude," for everything you can possibly think of. Doing so will increase the number of things you have to be grateful for.

**The power is within you. Your thoughts create your future. What are you thinking of, right now?**

# 12: Wealth and Spirituality

*Everyone plants, and everyone reaps from what they have planted. If you want wealth and happiness, be generous, and the Universe will be generous with you.*

*"There is no way to prosperity. Prosperity is the way."*

**Wayne Dyer**

## Spirituality and Wealth– Friends or Foes?

Recently, a woman hired me to help with her divorce. It was a contentious matter, and her future well being was under threat. She needed intensive dedicated legal service, and so, she hired me. I represented her as successfully as I have ever done for any client, and when we were all done, presented her with a bill for my services. She looked at me with utter surprise; then bitterness. Yes, she appreciated my work, but she assumed that since her cause was just, that I would work for free! All the joy in what we had accomplished was gone. All she could see was that she had been "screwed".

In my practice of holistic family law, I have sometimes attracted clients who are oriented to "spiritual values"; or at least, they think they are. For some reason, people like that tend (or pretend) to despise money as something dirty, and they pit spiritual values against the values of prosperity and wealth. That is like pitting earth against heaven!

Some people wrongly believe that wealth and prosperity are evil; or at least, that poverty is more "holy" than wealth. I don't know, but I think this view comes to us from Greek philosophy via medieval Christian theology. It certainly isn't in the Bible!

The most spiritual people in the Bible were the wealthiest men of their times: Job was renowned for his riches. Abraham, the "Father of faith" was a man of great wealth. Moses was in line for the throne of Egypt. David was an emperor; Solomon, the wealthiest king that had ever lived. The Twelve Disciples were well to do businessmen. When Jesus began his public ministry, wealthy women supported him financially. The earliest churches met, not in the catacombs, but in "basilicas"; that is, great mansions owned by wealthy members of the parish. Wealth is just a repository of human life energy. If you value human life, you must respect the wealth that our labors produce.

People who are poor often think negatively of those who are not, saying such things as "The rich are greedy" or "Rich people are crooks." The truth, however, is that the wealthy contribute far more to others; such as jobs, taxes, and charitable donations, than people who cannot see past their own immediate needs. By thinking poverty thoughts, poor people remain poor. By demonizing wealthy people, they ensure that they will not be among them. After all, who wants to see themselves as greedy, or a crook?

Having wealth conduces to works of compassion and mercy because it frees the mind to consider the needs of others. It also presents opportunities to invest our treasure in matters of deep and valid concern. "For where your treasure is, there your heart will be also."

Energy is a composite of thought forms that plays out on the landscape of our lives. Every thing in the universe is made up of energy in differing forms. Money is just another form of energy. Given enough of it, you can literally move a mountain; not a "metaphorical" mountain, but a real one!

And you can move metaphorical mountains with money too. So why do people believe it is more "spiritual" to have low energy and be unable to move off the couch than to be powerful and able to help ourselves and others?

I would rather be rich.

If you ask, most of us would say we want to be rich. I remember after my divorce, wanting prosperity to enter my life. Yet it resisted me. I couldn't understand why until a teacher urged me to write down a list of everything I had ever heard about money as a child.  I began to see the beliefs that were creating my reality.  Here are some examples:

"There's never enough money to go around."

"Money is "filthy lucre."

"Rich people are greedy."

"Rich people are crooks."

"Money doesn't grow on trees."

"Poor like Jesus."

"Do you think I'm made of money?"

"Money is the root of all evil".

Try writing down your own list.  When you finish, you will understand what has been holding you back from the abundance you deserve.

Recognize that abundance – whether it be clients, connections or cash – is all around you. The only reason it hasn't arrived at your doorstep is that some part of your mind is blocking it.  That is why we all need to constantly program our minds through affirmations that make us willing to receive good.

Are you ready to open the floodgates of prosperity in your life?  Review your list of negative beliefs about money.  Now, get a new sheet of paper and turn them around. Rewrite the same beliefs as positive affirmations about wealth.

For example, "There is never enough money" can become "I am a limitless being accepting from a limitless source in a limitless way."  While you rewrite these old, negative messages, say to yourself: "I am willing to move past my parents' limitations."

- **Affirm:** "Everything I need to know is revealed to me and everything I need comes to me, easily and effortlessly."

- **Confess:** "I am Divinely protected and guided. My way is made smooth and easy, and I rejoice that this is so."

- **Affirm:** "My net income is constantly increasing."

- **Declare:** "I am making great money in a job that challenges my creativity, working with and for people I appreciate, and who appreciate me."

Select one or two affirmations that resonate with you and write them 25 times a day for at least a week. Sing them like a song in the shower or when you exercise. Make friends with people who have money. Let money know that it is your friend.

I often invite friends to my home to play *CashFlow*, a game designed by Robert T. Kiyosaki and Sharon Lechter. It teaches how to get out of the rat race and become financially free.

How do you treat the money you do have? Do you stuff it in a sock? Is it balled up in your wallet or purse? If it is, straighten out those bills. Line them up in order and fold them as if they were friends that you care for.

Stuart Wilde in *The Money Bible* recommends spending several minutes intensely focusing on a dollar bill and noticing all the little details on it; the shrubs, the windows, the pillars, and so on. This serves to put positive attention on your money, and what you put your attention on expands and grows.

Do you hate bills? Some people see bills as threats. They aren't. Bills are simply proof that someone trusted you enough to expend time and energy to provide you a product or a service, knowing that you have the ability and the will to compensate them. Don't let your bills pile up! That creates a feeling of poverty. Pay them as soon as they come in. When you pay your debts, bless each bill with love. When you write your checks, give each one a little kiss and say to the creditor, "Thank you for trusting me." If you will do that, you will find yourself in a position to trust other people who enlist your efforts to provide valuable services. When they do, bill them! You will have earned it.

Abundance is wired into the universe. It is infinite and eternal, and your affirmations are the seeds of a new harvest of happiness. Expose them to water, light, and air, and in time they will produce a harvest. If a tiny seed can produce sixty and one hundred fold, how much do you produce with your own thoughts?

Eric Butterworth, a minister and the author of *Spiritual Economics* says that each of us must ask for what we want in the Universe: We ask for water by turning on the tap. We ask for light by throwing the lamp switch. We ask for gravity to hold us in our seats by sitting upright and balanced. We don't make air. It is pressing to enter us at every point on our bodies. We invite it inside by simply opening our lungs, and allowing the abundance to rush in. Hope and prosperity are the symphonies which resound in the literature of every

> *Affirmation:*
>
> *I am an unlimited being receiving from an unlimited Source in an unlimited way. I am abundantly blessed beyond my fondest dreams. My net income is constantly increasing.*

religious tradition. The antiphonal theme is, "Ask and receive, sow and reap."

Jesus taught his disciples, "It is your Father's good pleasure to give you the kingdom." *Luke 12:32.* The Bible also says, "Prove me now, herewith, saith the Lord of Hosts, and I will open you up the windows of heaven and pour you out a blessing you have not room enough to receive." *Malachi 3:10.* Don't insult the Divine Source by asking for crumbs. Acknowledge today that you deserve all good, and are ready to receive.

Genuine gratitude opens the floodgates for more of what is good to come inside; but what I am talking about here is not the kind of gratitude that exists as a matter of policy, such as, "People in Africa are starving. Finish your peas!" No. I am referring to the kind of gratitude that is based on recognizing the incredible deal that you have just to be alive today.

The first step in cultivating genuine gratitude is to begin each day by acknowledging the good things in your life that day. Then, open your eyes to the plenty in everything around you. See the abundance of clouds in the sky; flowers in the fields, and leaves on the trees. Is it winter? Look out at the millions of snowflakes. Open your freezer and look at the food you have stored there. Open your closet. Look at the selection of warm and colorful clothing from which you have to choose your daily dress! Each day, open your arms as wide as you can and say: "I am open and receptive to all the good and abundance of the Universe." If it doesn't feel real, say it again, louder, and with more feeling. Say it again! It will become true for you in time. Now, as you address your tasks of the day, see them for what they are: Your chance to meet someone else's needs, and thereby participate in the prosperity that fills the world. End each day by acknowledging five things you have accomplished. Keep a journal and write them down. When you feel impoverished, look over your journal and see the many blessings there are in your life. Genuine gratitude will yield a continuing harvest of good!

# 13: What You Get Is What You See

WHAT MATTERS MOST IS HOW YOU SEE YOURSELF.

*I have a picture on my desk that inspires me whenever I go to court. It is a photograph of a kitten looking into a mirror, seeing its reflection as a tiger. The caption says "Never underestimate the power of a strong self image." Physical appearance does not determine the success of our endeavors. Success is determined by how we choose to see ourselves.*

## "Mirror, Mirror on the Wall; Who's the Fairest One of All?"

*Snow White* opens with a queen who rules the realm. Despite this awesome power, her sense of her own value is so weak she has to consult a magic mirror every day for reassurance that she is the "fairest in the land"--whatever that means. Time passes, and one day the charmed glass reports to her that someone else is fairer than she. The queen resolves to have her rival killed. Such is the premium that vanity assigns to the contours of a face. This is the poverty mentality at its worst;

the belief that we are diminished by what someone else has.

Every day, women all over the world look into a not-so-magic mirror and criticize the image they see. We all do it. Perhaps we focus on a too-wide mouth, a long nose, a blemish, or the appearance of unwelcome lines. "If only I looked like (fill in the blank)," we think, "I would be OK."

Whenever we compare ourselves to stars in the entertainment media, we tend to come up short. Why? We are comparing our insides to other people's air-brushed outsides. We are being asked to strive for unattainable ideals. The deck is stacked.

I recently looked under my own bathroom vanity. There, I found all manner of lavish creams, exotic oils, and imported lotions which I had accumulated over the years. Each of them had a different label holding forth the same basic promises—heightened erotic appeal, enhanced beauty, and everlasting youth. Taking inventory, I realized that they had been there for years. I must have believed the labels, because I bought them all. I truly thought that beauty and happiness came from outside of me.

Each year, the cosmetics industry spends billions to persuade us that we do not merit love unless we buy their wares. Pop culture teaches that our lives would be happier and more exciting if we did not have to work for our livelihood. Television and movies lead us to believe that even the most complex life dramas can be resolved within a couple of hours. All of them focus on deep needs that we all have then create the illusion that they have the solution to meet those needs. This, however, is not true. The power is within us. Usually, we just don't realize it.

We think that we know ourselves, but the truth is we can't even see ourselves. In order to get to where we want to go, we have to know where we are right now. Thus, to experience a happier life takes looking into our own "magic mirror." The Universe has provided us with these wonderful mirrors; the reflection of the people around us. Do you want to know what you believe about yourself? Take a look at the people who surround you.

Do your loved ones honor and respect you? Or are you surrounded by people who reject you, belittle you, and tell you that it is for your own good? How others treat you closely matches how you treat yourself.

Mirror, mirror on the wall, are these experiences teaching you anything at all?

Are you with someone who constantly criticizes and ridicules you and everything else? This is most likely a reflection that you criticize and ridicule yourself. Are you with someone who is angry and fearful? This is an expression of your own anger and fear. Change your friends, kick your lover to the curb; get another job. You will attract the same people with different names.

The philosopher Voltaire wrote a novel *Candide* about a man who kept running into the same crazy people until he took stock of himself. He then made the oft-quoted realization: "We all must cultivate our own gardens."

People come into our lives because we attract them, for one reason or another. The people we like reflect the loving aspects of ourselves. The people we dislike reflect patterns within us that we need to change. If you find yourself blaming others or getting frustrated by what others do, take a moment and step back. Ask yourself what lesson this person is teaching you. We are all here to teach and to learn. Once you are willing to learn the lesson that you need to learn, and change, then the people who irritate you will either treat you differently, or they will move on.

In my earlier life I always seemed to attract the attentions of men who did not appreciate my abilities and talents. I tried and tried to win their admiration, but I never could. I worked to look perfect, speak perfectly, act appropriately, and do everything correctly. Yet I could not please them.

As I began my spiritual journey I went out into nature one day to find answers to this problem. I was at a week-long teacher training for Louise Hay's Love Yourself, Heal Your Life workshops in San Diego, California, and I went outside to gaze at the rows of sailboats in the nearby harbor. Specifically, I sought to understand how I could forgive a particular man who had treated me badly. As I reflected, I realized that my anger at the man who was unkind to me was like a sailboat getting angry at the water because the boat did not like its own reflection. Taking the analysis further, I realized that whatever water the sailboat found itself in; its reflection would be the same. The only way the sailboat's reflection would change, would be for the boat itself to change. The water was just passively reflecting, not creating, an image.

We teach people how to treat us by what we will accept from them. As I learned to love and appreciate my own unique qualities, the critical, unappreciative men moved out of my life. No fuss, no drama. Instead of being eaten alive with bitterness, I valued these relationships for the lessons which have enriched my life. When I learned the lesson, they moved on.

Try this experiment: Think of someone in your life who annoys you. Write down everything about that person that irritates you. Now, sit quietly. Look into that "magic mirror" on the wall of your consciousness. Ask yourself where in your life you do the very same things. You will be amazed to find that somewhere in your life you do every one of the things that are being done to you.

The goal of this experiment is a higher state of self awareness. To achieve that goal, you must avoid the temptation to indulge in self criticism. Self-awareness liberates us to achieve our highest good. Criticism only locks us into the very patterns we want to change. Know that you are doing the very best you can in this moment. And so is everyone else. Make this affirmation: "I am willing to release the need to be critical of myself and others." The development of self awareness will bear its own fruits.

The first step to power is the achievement of clarity. Therefore, you deserve to acknowledge yourself for being willing to change. If you have come that far, then you are doing the very best you can in this moment.

Try wearing a rubber band around your wrist for a few days. Every time you criticize yourself or someone else, snap the rubber band against your wrist. Notice how often you say, "ouch." When you criticize internally, it disturbs your sense of well-being. The rubber band helps "snap" you out of the habit.

The longer you blame your spouse, your parents, or your siblings for the problems apparent in your life, the more you give away your own power. Blaming others for your misfortunes won't help. Acknowledge that you are 100% responsible for whatever happens in your life, and watch how powerful you become.

As you begin each day, be on the lookout for ways to love your Self. Look deeply into your own eyes in the mirror and say, "I love you." Praise yourself for every little thing you accomplish:

- "I stood up to a bully today."

- I wrote out an exercise regimen and clarified fitness goals.

- "I cleaned out a workspace that I have been putting off for months."

Each step forward will bring you more joy.

### *Affirmation:*

*I willingly release the need to criticize myself and others. I love and accept myself, exactly as I am now.*

As you learn these new patterns of thinking, be patient with yourself. You are planting seeds, and seeds take time to grow. If you persevere, you will be surprised how many times you look into the mirror and see a smile beaming back at you. Soon, you will reap a harvest of happiness.

# 14: Meeting Yourself on the Path

*Life is a journey that sometimes brings us full circle. Some people walk the same path until their feet wear a deep trench in the ground. Others step out of their rut and set off for new adventures. There is risk, but there is also reward.*

*Better a diamond with a flaw than a pebble that is perfect.*

Confucius

## All Diamonds Start Life as a Chunk of Coal and Work Their Way Up

Whenever I tried to communicate with one particular lawyer, her responses were cold, uncooperative, and even hostile. At one point she hurled a tirade of outrageous accusations at me. She made slanderous statements about me in court – including a claim that I sent my client to a "faith healer." I was already upset. After a year of hard work on a tough divorce case, my client had replaced me at the very end with another lawyer, to avoid paying her bill. In my place she hired this combative woman who assailed my professionalism in open court. In 17 years of practicing law I had never been accused of breaching ethics. But there I was, embarrassed and shamed amid my peers.

What had I done? I had an emotionally needy client who was racking up hours on the telephone looking to me for emotional support that was really beyond a lawyer's ability to give, and certainly not cost effective to her. What she needed was therapy, and so I sent her to a Reiki Master who used healing touch to soothe her nerves and help her regain her composure. Reiki practitioners undergo several levels of training and certification, and this particular individual was among the finest. Nevertheless, the other lawyer acted as if this Master were a snake oil salesman. As she portrayed it, I was a "flake" because I ran a spiritually oriented, holistic law firm that sought to uplift clients and resolve their conflicts from the inside out. Here I was, being pilloried for trying to help! She had slandered my character, and I was going to have to put her in her place! It was all-out war. So much for the win-win solution! I couldn't stop thinking about the courtroom scene; it woke me up in the middle of the night, to furiously scribble retaliatory motions against my accuser.

Have you ever been in a situation like this, where you had to choose between bitterness or simply learning the lesson that comes from the crisis? There are no mistakes, and there is a reason why everything happens when it does. Happily for me, this time, wisdom prevailed, and I received the gift from the experience.

Browsing a bookstore I found the help I needed; *Crucial Conversations: Tools for Talking When Stakes are High*, by Kerry Patterson, Joseph Grenny, Ron McMillan, and Al Switzler. A few pages into this text, and the message came through loud and clear.

According to these authors, the most successful people are those who can think clearly during crucial encounters, when the adrenaline is flowing and the charging bull ready to rage. Who can think straight when your heart is pumping reserves to organs ready to do battle or flee?

Those who can achieve calm in these challenging moments find themselves respected in the workplace, and happy in long-term marriages. Clearly, the real success in life comes from peace within, not just acquisitions of titles and cash. Yet the authors of this book say most of us in such moments take refuge in some form of silence: masking, avoiding or withdrawing. Or violence: controlling, labeling and attacking the accuser.

Being a holistic lawyer, I was sure this would not apply to me; but just to be sure I went to the web and took their mini-test.

The results? I demonstrated five of the silence tactics, and six of the violence tactics, for a total of 11 out of 12 negative responses to crisis!

Who, Me? **"Yes, YOU,"** said my inner wisdom gently.

Yikes! The light went on. I began to understand why the gift of this confrontation had happened to me, at this time in my life. For the first time, I saw how much these tactics had hurt me in my past relationships, and how my life would continue to improve as I learned new techniques for dealing with conflict. Because of this harsh experience, I was ready to move to a new level of understanding, and "walk the talk" with deeper authenticity.

The authors suggest that in a crisis situation, we should ask three critical questions before letting emotions take hold:

1. What do I want for myself?

2. What do I want for others? And

3. What do I want for this relationship?

Remembering these values in a crisis prevents us from being distracted by ego-related issues such as our wounded pride, or our desire to defeat our enemy. These impulses are just emotional interference, which sidetracks us from true resolution.

*A Course in Miracles* teaches that there are only two emotions: love and fear. When someone attacks us, they are acting from fear, or "safety concerns." When we attack back, so are we. The only way to resolve a conflict is to get back into dialogue, soul to soul. The only way to get back into dialogue is to notice when safety is at risk. This is the time to step out of the content of the conversation, establish safety for all the participants, and then return to the discussion.

Does this sound easy? I wouldn't call it easy, since the ego-warrior in me stands ready to attack like a ravenous dog at the slightest provocation. (She is a scary person to meet on the path!) But I am willing to change, and I am open and receptive to learning how to communicate in ways that build up everyone with whom I interact.

## *Affirmation:*

*I release the need to be right.*

*I am willing to see my flaws and correct them as needed.*

*I am a spiritual being having a human experience.*

*All is well, and I am safe.*

As I pondered these thoughts I've booked myself an appointment with that same Reiki Master.

By being willing to face and accept my flaws, I become more of the diamond I am meant to be. Let peace start from within and flow outward to the world.

## Becoming a Diamond Requires Going Through the Pressure Cooker

A diamond is a lump of coal that goes through incredible pressure and stress in order to become the dazzling sought-after jewel which we so highly value. Make a list of the situations in your life that cause you pressure and stress. Don't run from them! Face them calmly and without resistance to see where you are a part of the problem. Be willing to see your flaws, knowing that your ability to acknowledge them is the key to the solution.

Since we can't change anyone but ourselves, learning to see our own flaws is the key to gaining power in these tough situations. Once we change our reactions or ourselves, the situation will change.

People who do not honor us will move out of our lives. Situations that cause us stress will either alleviate, or we will perceive them differently. Making others wrong simply turns us into a victim, and victims have no power. They are always subject to the whims of others.

By being willing to see our own flaws, we allow the pressure to transform us from a simple lump of coal into the beautiful diamond we are meant to be!

# 15:
# Earn Emotional Freedom
# With Intuitive Choices

*"Did you ever have to make up your mind –*
*say yes to one and leave the other behind?"*
*sang the Lovin' Spoonful. Every day we are*
*bombarded with choices for what to do with*
*our time - watch television, read a book, visit*
*a relative, complete a work assignment, play*
*with our kids, exercise or lounge on the beach.*
*The choices we make shape our lives.*

You must master
your time rather
than becoming a
slave to the
constant flow of
events and demands
on your time. And
you must organize
your life to achieve
balance, harmony,
and inner peace.
                    *Brian Tracy*

## Laws of Success

Each choice carries with it a certain anxiety – "Is this the right decision - or would another choice be better?" In the Seven Spiritual Laws of Success, Deepak Chopra says, "The best way to understand and maximize the use of karmic law is to become consciously aware of the choices we make in every moment."

I came face-to-face with the impact of decision making one 4th of July. On the day America declares its freedom, I realized I was free to make a choice between preparing for a court case or enjoying my father's company. Which choice would make me feel better inside? Which would serve the higher interest?

On the one hand, I had a particularly vexing case that was crying for my attention. A former client had hired an aggressive attorney to seize back all the money she paid in legal fees, and was trying to do so by lambasting my character in court. (See chapter 14.) On the other hand, my father was 80 years old. He and my aunt had just traveled unexpectedly from Wisconsin for the first time in years. Dad has a delightful sense of humor that always lifts my spirits. My children also enjoy his company. Right there within my grasp I had a rare chance to reminisce about family and share a barbecue with him.

What criteria would I use to make the decision? At stake, I perceived, was my reputation in the legal community, and some substantial legal fees, which I had worked very hard to earn. If my criterion was my own sense of status among my professional peers, I would have surely rejected the opportunity to visit with Dad. If securing the money were absolutely critical, I'd do what was necessary to defend my fees. Truthfully, it was a lot of money.

After some reflective thought, I chose to spend the day with Dad. Why? Because I chose to listen to my Higher Self, rather than to my ego. Deepak Chopra says, "You and I are essentially infinite choice-makers. In any moment of our existence, we are in the field of all possibilities where we have access to an infinity of choices."

All attorneys are under contract to provide legal services to their clients. In contentious divorce cases, lawyers almost always end up very deeply engaged in the client's personal experience. Some clients have problems with boundaries. In this particular situation, I was being sued by a former client who had become a human vacuum, sucking up time and emotional energy like a tractor engine sucks fuel. After my service was given, she disputed the fees and wanted her money back. I exhausted an additional $5,000 trying to prove myself right against someone who often makes everyone around her wrong. By the time Dad showed up unexpectedly, I had begun to obsess about how to restore my wounded pride. My inner voice led the way, and the choice was to stay in harmony with my family and release my feelings about the court case.

I made the right choice. My aunt brought a scrapbook of family memories - of 4th of July picnics past when the whole family attended. Dad and I had one of our best times ever. We shared a leisurely lunch; then painted together, until the guest bathroom became a lovely shade of French coffee. To celebrate our handiwork, we shared a cup of homemade cappuccino that was the same color as the walls.

I am grateful that I chose wisely. In an afternoon of laughter, paintbrushes and faded pictures, I reconnected with my past, rooted myself securely to my family in the present, and poised myself to stand solidly in the future.

Robert Putnam, a Harvard University political scientist and author of the book, *Bowling Alone: America's Declining Social Capital,* suggests that society has become more and more disconnected from itself. Between 1972 and 1994, the number of people saying they spent a social evening with a neighbor at least once per week dropped from 22.1 percent of all respondents to 16 percent. The number of people who attend Parent Teacher Association meetings dropped from 12 million in 1964 to 7 million in 1994.

One thing we know from such glaring statistics is that people who disengage from family, church and social interactions in the neighborhood and at schools, are people who seldom trust - even their doctor, who may have their best interests at heart. They may not experience value, even when a miracle occurs in their midst.

That's why I chose holistic law in the first place. I wanted to help people become empowered in their lives, not just make myself richer for having won a case. The more I seek to enrich the quality of my life and of those around me, the more we all win in the universal courtroom.

I can't be attached to a certain result in this one case. It is the journey that matters more because I lead by example. I already have an abundant supply of good clients who respect my legal counsel and pay for my services gladly. Clients will always be there so long as I serve them well. I don't know how long I'll have my father's companionship.

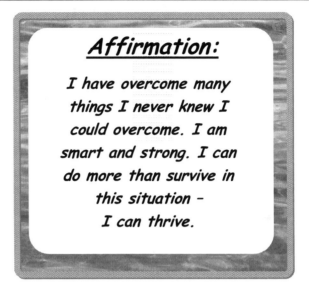

*Affirmation:*

*I have overcome many things I never knew I could overcome. I am smart and strong. I can do more than survive in this situation – I can thrive.*

## Family is a Choice

Make a list of the things that take up the most time in your life. Are they causing you stress and draining your energy? If so, let them go! Look at what you can do to encourage relationships and create harmony between you, your family, and your life. This strengthens your body, and your mind.

Make a journal of your decisions. Record them, so you can look back on them and see how your life has changed. Repeat as necessary.

# 16:
# Win-Win Divorce:
# An Oxymoron?

Americans have become jaded on the subject of divorce, and it's no wonder: The National Center for Health Statistics reports that in 2006, there were 48 divorces for every hundred marriages that occurred.

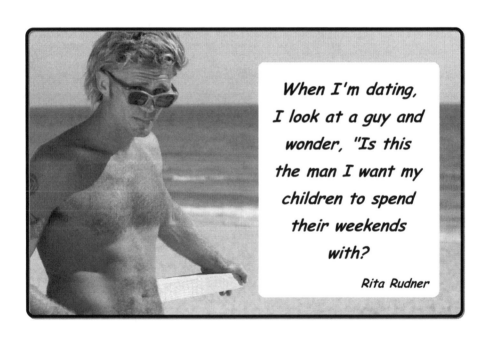

*When I'm dating, I look at a guy and wonder, "Is this the man I want my children to spend their weekends with?*

Rita Rudner

## The Reality of Divorce

There are more divorced people than married people in America today. As a result, some have become cynical about love and marriage. Others, who see divorce as a mythic tragedy, become obsessed with their own case, thinking or talking of nothing else, to the dismay of their families and friends, who either avoid them or die of boredom. As a holistic divorce lawyer, I say it's time for a pragmatic approach to what has become a fact of life; marriages often fail.

You may think that the statistics on divorce are good news for me. As a family law attorney I make my living representing people in divorce. Just think; all that new business!

Fortunately, I see a much bigger picture than that. Why? I was the child of a bitter divorce myself. I remember spending my childhood in my dark bedroom, terrified, because that was when Mom and Dad had their worst arguments. In my own divorce, I experienced the fear and uncertainty of starting over. For these reasons, I am passionate about helping people see divorce as a doorway to an extraordinary life. I know that it's possible. I've done it myself.

Here are four simple steps you can take to be the winner in your divorce:

**Step One:** **Release the Need to Blame**

Whenever we blame someone else for what happens in our life we give our power away. This may seem hard to accept at first. But as Dr. Kimberly Ventis-Darks says, "There are no victims, only volunteers. We teach people how to treat us by what we will accept from them." That is why it is so very important to release the need to blame your spouse for whatever went wrong in your marriage.

The good news is that when we take 100% responsibility for everything that happens in our lives, we begin to have real power. This does not mean condoning someone's poor behavior. It simply means recognizing our part in creating a situation that allowed it to happen in our experience.

**Step Two:**    **Refuse to Criticize Yourself**

Sometimes, instead of blaming our spouse, we attack ourselves instead. While blame takes us right out of the zone of power, self criticism actually locks us into the very pattern we are trying to change.

Think of the last time you criticized yourself; for example, your body image. How long have you been criticizing your body? Your eating? Your exercise habits? Forever, right? What kind of improvements has that practice brought you? Don't tell me. I already know the answer.

In truth, criticism and blame are smoke screens that block us from seeing the lesson that will take us to the next level. Remember the "magic" of mistakes when you are going through a divorce, and refuse to criticize yourself, NO MATTER WHAT! Remember, you did not come into this world to change anyone else. You are here to heal your own life. This brings me to the third step:

**Step Three:**   **Be Willing to See the Lesson**

Once we rub the smoke out of our eyes, the lesson we need to learn will be waiting for us, a shining gift. You may not see yours immediately, but do not worry. All you need is a little willingness, and the Universe will do the rest.

You may think, "That's easy for you to say. You don't know what I'm going through. You don't feel the pain I'm feeling." It's true, no one else can feel your pain. And that's just as well, because each person has their own issues that are uniquely suited to their ability to bear. I have lived five decades, and had my own share of difficulties, like everyone else. When I learned to stop blaming my parents, and understood that they were doing the best they could with the knowledge, information, and awareness that they had, my introspection became an outlook. When I learned to stop criticizing myself for staying in a bad marriage so long, I began to ride my horse in the direction it was going. Forward!

There are no mistakes. There is a reason you are going through everything you are going through. So be gentle and patient with yourself, and reduce your fear level with knowledge:

**Step Four:** **Knowledge Is Power**

The court's basic goals in your divorce will be an equal distribution of assets and child custody arrangements that are in the best interests of the children. There is only so much that the courts will allow. The more you learn about what can and cannot be accomplished, the more money you will save, and the more peace of mind you will have.

That is why this is no time to hide our heads in the sand! Take the initiative to find out all you can. There are some very fine seminars you can attend that will give you an understanding of the basics of divorce. There are also many helpful resources available on the Internet. For example, our website, www.lady4justice.com, offers a wealth of information on various aspects of divorce. Check us out!

I myself followed each of the steps I am suggesting to you. The change did not happen overnight, but I persisted. When we follow universal laws the results are inevitable. By honoring them I transformed my life. Now, for the first time, I have a happy home and a life that works. My approach to divorce was the springboard that took me to a higher level. It can work for you, too.

## *Affirmation:*

*Today is a new day.*
*I am a new me.*
*I think differently.*
*I act differently.*
*Others treat me differently.*
*All my changes are easy to make.*

## Start Your Adventure

Start each day with the decision to praise yourself for every little thing and not to criticize yourself, no matter what! Visualize your mind as calm water where peaceful insights bubble up. As you calmly release negativity, welcome the insights that reveal where you can do things more productively.

So often we take our successes for granted because we do not think they are good enough. Yet if we do not appreciate what we have, how can we ever get more? Look back to where you were last year. Acknowledge yourself for how far you have come. If you do this quick "reality check" from time to time you will be amazed at your progress!

Appreciate yourself. Acknowledge yourself. Accept yourself, just as you are, right now. Your journey has only just begun.

# 17: Move Into the Winning Circle

*When an airplane is lost in a fog, the only way to remain straight and level is to believe the gauges. The same is true in our life experience on the ground. When people consult their inner wisdom, they are better able to face challenges, because they are using their internal compass. There comes a time in everyone's life when they realize that giants lose their size if we stand up before facing them and call forth the giant within us.*

*"First, they ignore you. Second, they laugh at you. Third, they fight you. Finally, you win."*

*Gandhi*

## Challenges Come in All Shapes and Sizes – So Do Winners

Several years ago I had a challenging case against the largest law firm in the state. I tried first for the "win-win" solution, but their client was determined to punish my client and they would have none of it. Despite the big guns they were aiming at us, they really had no case. In that situation, I knew that the only course of action that remained was to stand firm.

My client was learning to overcome her fears and stand up for herself for the first time in her life. The truth was her defense, and she really wanted me to be her lawyer. I could not let her down. So I took the case, and told her to be ready for a fight.

There ensued a heated litigation battle that kept me up some nights until 4:30 AM, and busy many weekends. Sometimes, I made mistakes. Sometimes, our efforts failed; but as Winston Churchill once said "Courage is the ability to go from failure to failure without losing your enthusiasm." So we fought with courage, and even though we didn't win all of our battles along the way, we never lost our enthusiasm.

I have not always been courageous. In fact, I used to let fear control me so much that I stayed in a bad marriage for 23 years, because I feared the alternative. When the marriage ended, I was 46 years old, starting over with teenage twins, unsure of myself and even more afraid than I would have been had I taken the leap years before. Still, I trusted the inner voice that told me it was necessary to move forward alone.

Here is what Helen Keller had to say about playing it safe in *The Open Door:*

*"Security is mostly superstition. It does not exist in nature, nor do the children of men as a whole experience it. Avoiding danger is no safer in the long run than outright exposure."*

Studies show that 85% of people allow fear of failure to outweigh their desire to succeed. When they do, of course, failure is guaranteed.

People who are visionaries, who have dreams, do not go through life playing it safe. The fact is, there's no safe position in life! We're can't get out of life alive. We have to die to leave here! When I realized this, I decided it was time for me to start living my dream. So I forgot about playing it safe, and decided to take some risks.

It is said that people die at age 21, but they're not buried until age 65. Don't let that happen to you. Do you have a dream? If you don't, I want you to make one up. Then write it down and say to your Self, "It's possible."

Faith in the achievability of our dreams is the first essential to their realization. The second step is this: You have to realize that it's hard. Realizing a dream is no cakewalk. It takes training and preparation. You will make mistakes, and you will experience failures.

There is a saying that anything worth doing is worth doing right. This is obvious; but it is even more true that anything worth doing is worth doing badly until you get it right. Like babies, we must crawl before we learn to walk.

Most of us are afraid of making mistakes because we fear the censure of our peers. We are so afraid of derision that we give up on ourselves, because we are afraid someone will laugh at us if we try and fail.

If you want to achieve a dream, you must let this fear go. Don't worry about mistakes; you're going to make mistakes. Don't worry about failure. Make failure your friend. Learn to fail forward. Don't just pick yourself up. Pick yourself up, learn from your mistake, adjust, and move forward. Above all, keep this in mind: It's not over until you WIN!

The poet Goethe observed that until one is committed, there is hesitancy; the chance to draw back. Whatever your dream is, you must start BEFORE you are ready. The only way to succeed at your goal is to pull out all the stops, and get started, whether you're ready or not. There is nothing so powerful as a made-up mind. Don't ask how you're going to accomplish it. Boldness has power and magic in it! "How" you're going to do it is none of your business! If the "Why" is big enough, the "How" doesn't matter. It will be revealed. Define your dream; then leap, and the net will appear.

In my court case, the "downtown" lawyers laughed at me when I made mistakes. They tried to intimidate me with their numbers and their resources. Who was I, a solo practitioner and a woman at that, to come up against this massive law firm? The answer was simple. I was one individual who had an absolute belief in my client, and the determination to continue until her cause prevailed.

It didn't matter that the court moved the trial date up at the last minute, leaving me just two days to prepare. The opponent's entire legal team was scrambling; as a solo I put in 15-hour days with just a few hours' sleep! But when a person decides she believes in what she's doing, and refuses to quit, nothing can stop her. Our legal opponents realized that. They came in and asked the court to dismiss their case, on the morning of trial. In the end, we prevailed decisively. We had a goal, and we reached it. And we got them to reimburse my client for all the attorney fees she had paid, to boot.

People who aim at nothing end up hitting their target, dead on the head. Don't let that be you. In order to win, you must have a target; the ultimate success of your goal.

Every one of us has unique gifts to offer the world. If you don't share your gifts, the world will suffer for it. Don't die with your music still in you. Let your song be heard!

Write down your goal. Look at it and think about it every day. Decide that you're going to be fired up about your dream, and go at it with all your resources! Don't doubt that you have what it takes, for the truth is, we all have greatness within us.

Helen Keller said, **"Life is either a daring adventure or nothing."** Make your life a daring adventure. Find your dream, realize that it's possible for you to achieve it, and acknowledge that it won't be easy. Most importantly, decide, "It's not over, until I WIN!"

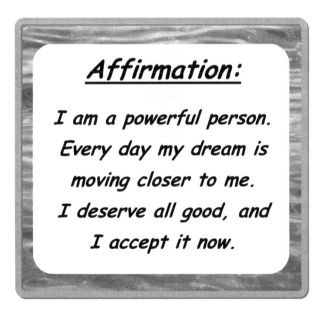

*Affirmation:*

*I am a powerful person.*
*Every day my dream is*
*moving closer to me.*
*I deserve all good, and*
*I accept it now.*

## Life is an Adventure

The ability to celebrate our smallest success, prepares us to climb the highest mountain. Learn to climb mountains, not stare at them. Prepare yourself to succeed.

You have just read this book. That is a serious first step. Now, resist the urge to think about where you will be a year, a month, or even a week from now. Take one principle or exercise, and implement it in your life today. Learn to identify each day's successes and celebrate them. Remember this formula: Action, feedback, correction. Over and again, until you reach your goal.

1725600